Global Nuclear Disarmament
Geopolitical Necessities

Global Nuclear Disarmament
Geopolitical Necessities

Editor

V .R. Raghavan

DELHI POLICY GROUP   **VIJ BOOKS INDIA PVT LTD**

Published by

Vij Books India Pvt Ltd
(Publishers, Distributors & Importers)
2/19, Ansari Road, Darya Ganj
New Delhi - 110002
Phones: 91-11-43596460, 91-11-47340674
Fax: 91-11-47340674
www.vijbooks.com
e-mail : vijbooks@rediffmail.com

Table of Contents

Introduction

The Delhi Policy Group conducted an 18 month project on *Pathways to Nuclear Disarmament* held between 2010 and 2012. This was facilitated by the Nuclear Security Project of the Nuclear Threat Initiative (NTI), Washington D.C. The nuclear disarmament initiatives proposed by Schultz, Perry, Kissinger and Nunn (*Quartet*), and the developments in the disarmament - proliferation field in 2009-2010, formed the basis of the project. It brought together varying positions taken by governments, international non-government groups and reputed scholars to find viable routes to disarmament.

The Project was implemented through seminars, workshops and round tables/lectures. The unique feature of the project activity was the screening of the film "Nuclear Tipping Point" in various parts of India amongst the civilian and defence population alike. Three international seminars were conducted on thematic issues in an effort to deepen the understanding on the pathways to nuclear disarmament concept of *Base Camp* and *Mountain Top*, as well as examining the common ground within existing commitments and proposals made on disarmament. The specific focus of each of the three seminars conducted was:-

Nuclear Disarmament: Time Line Challenge:. Several important issues had emerged in the wake of the push for disarmament initiatives by the *Quartet*, by President Obama's speech in Prague and his Administration's initiatives through the QDR and Nuclear Posture Review, etc. These issues are related to the lower arsenal levels which can be reached by nuclear weapons states and the speed with which such levels can be attained. An important dimension related to the concept of *Basecamp* which was the starting point for the route to lower arsenals, leading ultimately to the elimination of nuclear weapons. The *Basecamp* concept would of necessity include lower arsenal levels and time lines needed to reach them. In addition, key variables which were to influence the process of reaching smaller arsenals were examined. These included among others, variables like control of the production of fissile material; operational posture of weapons; declaratory policy; fuel cycle capabilities; security and monitoring weapons-usable material etc.

The speakers at this seminar were Dr. Sverre Lodgaard who delivered the keynote address followed by presentations by Ambassador T.P. Sreenivasan and Dr. G. Balachandran.

Doctrinal Challenges to Nuclear Disarmament: The key policy documents of Obama's administration like the Quadrennial Defence Review, Nuclear Posture Review etc. have shown the difficulties posed by military doctrines in proceeding apace on disarmament. The salience of nuclear weapons in military doctrine of nuclear weapon states requires a comparative analysis to arrive at a better understanding of the relationship between the imperatives of disarmament and the determinants of military doctrine. This is particularly relevant in an era in which, as per President Obama while the risks of nuclear war have reduced, the dangers of a nuclear strike have increased.

The keynote address was delivered by Dr. Bruno Tertrais, followed by paper presentations by Ambassador Jacek Bylica, Dr. Swaran Singh and Lt. Gen. Prakash Menon.

Nuclear Disarmament: Geopolitical Imperatives: The current interpretations of Nuclear Zero are both varied and confusing. These range from zero nuclear weapons to zero possibility of a nuclear war being used with a number of possibilities in between. Some even interpret fewer nuclear weapons, possibly a hundred or less, as amounting to zero. The examination of different interpretations of Zero and their consequences on the disarmament outlook originally listed by the *Quartet,* produced an energised disarmament debate.

The seminar had presentations by Dr. Ian Anthony, Dr. Sheel Kant Sharma and Mr. Alexander Kolbin.

Delhi Policy Group is proud to be associated with NTI and Nuclear Security Project in sustaining the discourse on nuclear disarmament.

Pathways to Nuclear Disarmament: Timeline Challenges

Sverre Lodgaard

Introduction

In order to explain the topic, two caveats are in order. First, for political leaders to act on complex realities, the realities have to be simplified. Heuristic assumptions to that effect may be flawed, but by making ambitious objectives more thinkable, decision-makers are more likely to pursue them. To convince governments that a Nuclear Weapon-Free World (NWFW) can be achieved, it is important to distinguish majors from minors and identify markers on the way, in the form of base camps and milestones. Second, visions can be powerful guides to action. When considering the pros and cons of specific arms control and disarmament measures, the attractiveness of the vision must be weighed in. The four American horsemen who revived the objective of a NWFW, stressed the interplay between vision and action: "without the bold vision, the actions will not be perceived as fair or urgent; without the actions, the vision will not be perceived as realistic or possible".[1] Therefore, the starting point should be the outlining of two different versions of the vision and a working from there to base camps, milestones, pathways to the milestones and back to the maze of the present.

Visions

The vision of a NWFW comes in several forms, one which imagines a world where all ready-made weapons have been eliminated, but where many states maintain a mobilisation base for reintroduction of them. This

---

[1] Shultz et al. (2007) 'A World Free of Nuclear Weapons', *The Wall Street Journal*, page A15. Available at http://www.fcnl.org/issues/item.php?item_id=2252&issue_id=54.

may include fissile materials in stock, able nuclear weapons, engineers and manufacturing equipment on hand and delivery vehicles, ready for use. For the Nuclear Weapon States (NWS), this would be a form of deep de-alerting, not much different from the status of Japan today. The purpose of the capability base is to deter others from breaking out of the agreement and to confront violators if deterrence breaks down.

Such a NWFW would be the logical end state of a dominant line of thought in US disarmament affairs: the more advanced the capacity for reconstitution, the more the nuclear arsenal can be cut. This is a world where the NWS would be without operative weapons, but remain nuclear capable. As the last nuclear weapons go away, some states would be virtual NWS, while a great majority of others would be without similar capabilities. For as long as the NPT is in force, the non-nuclear members are not allowed to engage in activities that are specifically weapons-related. In one particular respect, the lead of the established NWS is unavoidable: they are the ones having design and testing experience and that knowledge cannot be erased.

Different ground rules for different categories of states are hard to imagine, however. Fourty years of discontent with the NPT's division of the world into nuclear and non-nuclear weapon states and persistent complaints over the slow implementation of Art. VI, which was supposed to end it, have led many NNWS to insist on equal rules for all. Obama's Prague and Cairo speeches alluded to it.[2] In effect, the principle of equity is important all throughout the disarmament process: the majority of NNWS will protest any attempt to maintain the current imbalance in the implementation of the NPT; they will demand that single arms control and disarmament measures be equitable; they will do their utmost to ensure that capability differences are reduced as the process unfolds; and smaller nuclear powers will do their best to reign the bigger ones in. If the equity principle is compromised by moves for unilateral advantage on the part of the most advanced NWS, the emerging powers of Asia, in particular, are unlikely to be cooperative.

---

[2] For the Prague speech, see www.huffingtonpost.com/.../obama-prague-speech-on-nu_n_183219.html. The Cairo speech is available at http://www.whitehouse.gov/the_press_office/Remarks-by-the-President-at-Cairo-University-6-04-09

If the NWS disarm on the formula that "the stronger the reconstitution capabilities, the deeper the cuts", and the world of zero is based on equitable rules, NNWS will be free to emulate the same logic. Equity on the basis of ground rules that allow virtual arsenals may tempt many more states to exercise this option. Nuclear deterrence – latent or virtual rather than manifest – could become an option free for all, quite possibly leading to a multiplication of deterrence relationships. Especially if nuclear power stations and national fuel-cycle facilities proliferate, there may be many more threshold states. Reservations made for the path dependence of nuclear disarmament – always a big caveat – it could, at worst, lead to life in a virtual deterrence crowd. A world without nuclear weapons would not be a world without conflict, so tense relations may encourage hedging.

Virtual arsenals and the same rules for all are a dangerous combination. First, because it sustains the mentality that nuclear war is possible. Many states may come to think that hedging is prudent, suspecting that others may be cheating, leading to a hedging race: vertically toward capabilities that can be turned faster and faster from virtual to real; horizontally to involve more states. The trust on which abolition was achieved might evaporate. Second, virtual arsenals need arsenal keepers and they are never disinterested experts, but socio-political actors legitimising their activities in terms of threats to be met and demanding more resources to counter them. Far from being alien to hedging races, arsenal keepers would quite possibly prefer a return from virtual arsenals to real ones. Such an end state would therefore contain the seeds of its own destruction. Third, it is a particularly bad idea because in the break-out scenarios, first strike capabilities are more likely to emerge rather than in current nuclear constellations.[3]

It would, therefore, be better to go "below zero" to eliminate the fissile materials that have been dedicated to nuclear explosive uses; to institute strict international control of all remaining materials; to dismantle

---

[3] Harald Muller, 'The Importance of Framework Conditions' in G. Perkovich and J. Acton (eds) *Abolishing Nuclear Weapons: a debate*, Carnegie Endowment for Peace. Available at <http://www.carnegieendowment.org/files/Muller.pdf>

the nuclear weapons infrastructure; and to redirect the workforce to other sectors. Even more, nuclear materials that can be used to build weapons should be banned from civilian use as well. Highly Enriched Uranium (HEU) is not really the big issue – there is little HEU left in the civilian sector and what remains is being phased out – but plutonium continues to pose a problem. Technical fixes may or may not solve it: if not, a compromise would have to be struck to accommodate the civilian industry. Dual-capable production facilities for civilian use would remain, possibly based on proliferation-resistant technologies and certainly subject to international control. This would be a more stable NWFW building trust in a non-nuclear future. It would be a world where nuclear deterrence no longer applies.

Base camps

These worlds are not dichotomous, but should rather be seen as end points on one and the same scale. Going below zero is a matter of more or less, so this image of a NWFW comes in several variations. Sidney Drell and James Goodby, who argue that a reconstitution capability would be needed to deter breakout, are attentive to the concerns that such capabilities may invite a reconstitution race and therefore, produce its own instabilities: "A careful judgement will have to be made among nations of comparable technical capabilities regarding nuclear activities that would be reasonable to retain in a state of latency, as opposed to those that are impermissible because they would push the world dangerously close to a reconstitution race".[4] Activities, facilities and weapons-related items would have to be "tested during the run-up to the end state, when responsive nuclear infrastructures would be maintained on relatively small scales and under conditions of agreed transparency".[5] At that stage, it would be necessary to make a pause to determine what kind of a NWFW to go for, i.e. a base camp. Drell and Goodby suggest that it might be appropriate to stop at the level of 50-100 weapons to consider whether the conditions for a final leap onto nuclear weapon freedom are reassuring enough and to establish

---

[4] Sidney Drell and James Goodby, *A World without Nuclear weapons*. Stanford, CA: Hoover Institution Press, 2009.
[5] Drell and Goodby, op.cit.

what rules and regulations should apply at the destination. Another view notes that the powers that subscribe to minimum deterrence keep close to 200 nuclear weapons; that India and Pakistan may be going for forces in about the same range; and that Israel may already be there. This level may have been chosen for good reason, out of regard for strategic stability and may therefore, be a more appropriate interim halting point. If it is assumed that multilateral disarmament negotiations are to be heading for ceilings in the lower end of the minimum deterrence range, barring significant increases in any of the forces, because it would run against the declared aim of the exercise, the base camp would be established at the level of 100-200 weapons.

At that point, the continuation is hard to foresee, for the world will look much different from today's world. Indeed, it would be presumptuous to claim to know much about it. However, political order issues aside, some force constellations are known to be more unstable and dangerous than others. A few parameters may therefore be laid down to steer the process away from the greatest risks in the final approach to a NWFW.

This pertains, in particular, to the worlds immediately above and immediately below zero. The dangers of a world immediately below have been spelt out above. Similar dangers would exist in a world immediately above. At the level of, say, 30 nuclear weapons, the retaliatory capabilities may be in doubt. Some weapons may be destroyed by an attacker, others may be intercepted and yet others may not function as planned. As a result, first-strike propensities may be too great for comfort. It may lead to a surprise attack, hitting the enemy when his guard is down, or to inadvertent escalation when decision-makers begin to think that war can no longer be avoided.

It may therefore be wise to skip those transitional phases immediately above and immediately below zero and go from the base camp directly to a NWFW significantly below zero. That can be done by eliminating weapon-grade materials, dismantling dedicated nuclear infrastructure and redirecting nuclear weapon expertise *before* eliminating the remaining weapons. In other words, the stability of minimum deterrence postures would be maintained till the stability of a NWFW has been ensured. Then, and only then, would it be time to move from the base camp to the destination.[6]

Milestones

Before coming to the base camp where the final leap to nuclear weapon freedom would be considered, two interim milestones may be of particular significance. One in terms of weapons and one in terms of doctrines, or one in terms of hardware and one in terms of software.

Deep cuts

The hardware milestone is deep cuts leading to multilateral disarmament negotiations. If the US and Russia can agree on radical overall reductions of their nuclear forces, more is likely to follow. If not, the call for elimination may come to nought. To reduce Russia's reliance on nuclear weapons, threat perceptions must be alleviated. The US accounts for 45 per cent of world military expenditures; Russia for three[7]; so to wait for stronger Russian conventional forces to reduce the role currently assigned to their nuclear weapons makes little sense. Threat reduction means policies that can ease tensions along Russia's borders in Europe, the Caucasus and Central Asia. Other matters of contention are the US ballistic missile defence program and the emerging US conventional Prompt Global Strike capabilities. In the West, three different political cultures are at work: a Western European culture where Germany is the heavyweight, disposed for closer cooperation with Russia depending on political and economic developments there: an East European culture still marked by its recent history of subordination to the Soviets, but gradually moving closer to the rest of the EU; and an American culture, which currently translates into policies that are sensitive to Russian concerns, but which has controversial elements. The first one seems rather stable and predictable. The second one is likely to swing back and forth with changing governments on the way to closer EU integration. On the other hand, US culture bodes for political shifts of much greater

---

[6] Sverre Lodgaard, *Nuclear Disarmament and Non-Proliferation. Towards a Nuclear-Weapon-Free-World?*, Routledge, UK, 2011, Ch. 10.

[7] *SIPRI Yearbook 2009: Armaments, Disarmament and International Security.* New York: Oxford University Press, Inc.

consequence.

How deep do US and Russian cuts have to be to engage the other NWS in multilateral disarmament talks? If they go below 1000 operative weapons and put strict limits on their reserves while inviting the others to negotiate common ceilings, they may come to the table. Under the impact of major progress, multilateral negotiations may not have to wait till the leading ones have come down to the level of the smaller powers. But if they were to invite the others with proportional reductions in mind, so that the US and Russia would retain significantly larger arsenals than the others, it may go nowhere. China may be hard put in any case, lest the US and Russia have found a solution to the BMD and Global Strike programs that meets Chinese concerns as well.

The five must be at the multilateral disarmament table as a matter of course, but who else should be invited?

India is an emerging power on the global scene and will sooner or later be recognised *de jure* as a NWS. If a criteria-based approach is adopted in relation to the three states that never joined the NPT, asking them to abide by the commitments that India has undertaken plus an Art.VI obligation, signature of the CTBT and limitations on fissile material production while a FMCT is being negotiated – making this the condition for de jure recognition; the bar can be put higher or lower – only India may be able to live up to it. In that case, the table would be enlarged from five to six. However, to leave Pakistan out for reasons of international law, disregarding the politico-military realities of the subcontinent, is untenable. In the long run, policies are best when they are based on facts and not on fiction. On this note, there would be seven participants.

North Korea is a case of its own in all sorts of ways and should be treated separately. Israel's nuclear weapons' rationale is distinctly regional. It says it can accept a NWFZ in the Middle East when peace in the region has become a stable prospect, i.e. when all else has been solved. It does not admit to being a NWS, but since NNWS would also be invited to the table on a formula for regional representation, Israel would not necessarily have to declare. However, for material restraints to be applied, transparency is obviously needed. North Korea and Israel may best be addressed in their respective regional contexts.

No-First-Use

On the doctrinal side, the corresponding milestone is No-First-Use (NFU). NFU gives one function to nuclear weapons and one only: deterring others from using theirs. The US Nuclear Posture Review says that the US will work to establish the conditions for a transition to NFU.

Under credible doctrines of NFU, premeditated use of nuclear weapons is ruled out. Per implication, threats of use are ruled out as well. Attempts to use them for military or political gains are off the screen. Apart from whatever residual status gains that the weapons may be seen to yield, for the NWS, their value becomes negative, for there would still be a risk of nuclear war by human or technical error and that risk is first of all a risk for their possessors. If deterrence fails, they will themselves be the targets and prime victims of devastation.

Therefore, if the NWS adopt NFU postures they would no longer incite others to acquire nuclear arms. They would no longer stimulate proliferation by example, for there would be nothing attractive to emulate. For nuclear disarmament, this is of the essence. Proliferation to more states may derail the effort, for it would reconfirm the utility that governments still see in nuclear weapons. Furthermore, when the weapons become a liability, it adds realism to the disarmament corollary of NFU: nobody would need them if nobody had them.

A NFU agreement may include a provision branding first use of nuclear weapons as a crime against humanity. If NFU takes hold by unilateral action, as is more likely, the Security Council could be invited to issue such a declaration. That would send a message to recalcitrant NWS that are not permanent members of the Council. A non-use agreement on the model of the Geneva Protocol on chemical and biological weapons of 1925 would convey the same message: the effects of nuclear weapons are such that no civilized state or sane leader should or would use them. Like the Geneva Protocol, it would in practice be a NFU agreement. So why not phrase this doctrinal milestone as a prohibition of nuclear weapons use?

As long as nuclear weapons exist, the possessors need a doctrine to explain why they are kept. When reviving the objective of a NWFW, President Obama reassured his critics that a viable deterrent would be maintained. Prohibition of use is a taller order than NFU, for literally understood, it undercuts deterrence even if indirectly, it amounts to the same. Seemingly questioning the right to respond in kind, it puts a symbolic hurdle on top of what is required for NFU. While non-use is a commendable objective for public opinion mobilisation, it may create confusion about the right to retaliate and should therefore not be mixed with the call for NFU.

Existential deterrence [8] – the notion that the sheer existence of nuclear weapons is enough to deter others, no doctrine or explanation being needed – reflects the same basic thinking, but does not explicitly exclude threats or use against NNWS. To insulate the continued existence of nuclear weapons from the security considerations of NNWS, NFU doctrines are better. For NFU to be credible, the script must be confirmed by matching deployments. In Europe, under the Cold War that meant for instance, withdrawal of tactical nuclear weapons from the frontlines in order not to be tempted to use them before they might be overrun and lost. Today, this is less of a problem. The U.S. Presidential Initiatives of 1991/1992 did away with many of them, and others were withdrawn to rear locations.

NFU means low numbers of weapons in rear positions. However, long-range systems can be used with very high accuracy over a range of distances and can be re-targeted on short notice, so their use cannot be made unambiguous only in reference to geography and technology. Substantial reductions of force levels would alleviate the problem, but not eliminate it. The credibility of NFU doctrines would have to be judged on the basis of the totality of nuclear-related hardware and software and that, in turn, presupposes a high degree of military transparency. Still, the conclusions will hardly be clear-cut. In practice, there may be shades of grey.

Pathways to the milestones

As is usually the case with major undertakings, no single approach will do the trick. A combination of pathways is required, addressing the political

---

[8] See McGeorge Bundy, *Danger and Survival.* New York: Vintage Books, 1988.

order requirements of disarmament; pushing the illegality of nuclear weapon use; enhancing the illegitimacy of use; and putting the historical utility of nuclear weapons straight.

The political order pathway

The first milestone – US-Russian cuts leading to multilateral talks – does not presuppose any change of world order, but implies a distinct shift from antagonistic behaviour to relations based on cooperation and mutual restraint, reminiscent of the "European concert" after the Napoleonic wars. Controversial military problems regarding tactical nuclear weapons, missile defence and new long-range conventional weapons must be solved, which in turn, presupposes that contentious political questions like NATO's role and reach and other sensitive issues, along Russia's southern borders and toward Iran, are better managed to the satisfaction of both.

As for the second, both Russia and Pakistan are a long way from NFU. Pakistan is prepared for first use to stop deep Indian incursions into its territory. To turn the conventional imbalance into a force relationship where the defensive capabilities on both sides are stronger than the offensive capabilities on the other – a stable non-provocative relationship – is beyond grasp. Similar to Russia's relationship with the West, Pakistan will remain militarily inferior to India, so the way to a Pakistani NFU doctrine goes via resolution of the Kashmir problem and alleviation of threat images. Of course, regional force adjustments can also facilitate a Pakistani transition to NFU.

Israel is the hardest problem. The purpose of its nuclear force seems obvious: nuclear weapons may be used to stem advancing conventional forces, as a means of last resort if national survival is at stake. The Israelis say that they are ready for a nuclear weapon-free zone when peace has become a stable prospect, i.e. when all else has been solved. In the Middle East, that is a long-term ambition. In Northeast Asia, the predicament is much the same. There, too, there is a long way to go before all else has been settled and until then, the regime in Pyongyang may want to retain a nuclear deterrent as an ultimate insurance premium, like the Israelis.

The smallest and weakest NWS are therefore among the hardest to convert to NFU and nuclear disarmament. In the Middle East, South Asia and Northeast Asia, it can only be achieved through regional peace arrangements. To succeed, major power support is needed.

The legal pathway

NNWS are more vulnerable to use and threats of use than NWS. Where mutually assured destruction applies, resort to nuclear weapons is an ordained act of suicide while in relation to NNWS, the aggressor may get away with it. Non-aligned states have therefore called for an international convention committing the NWS not to use or threaten to use nuclear weapons against NNWS parties to the NPT, no qualifications added. While the US NPR may be conducive to a new SC resolution, containing stronger security assurances than those in Resolution 984,[9] it would take more to meet the non-aligned demand for an international convention.

NFU doctrines meet the same concerns. In addition, they are more relevant in the case of deep cuts and elimination scenarios because of their in-built disarmament logic. Negative security assurances to NNWS are primarily a part of the NPT bargain: NFU would be a major contribution both to disarmament and non-proliferation. The Geneva Protocol of 1925 prohibited the use of chemical and biological weapons. These weapons were considered inhuman. Later, possession of them was outlawed as well: biological weapons by the BWT of 1972; chemical weapons by the CWC of 1992 and the CWC set a timeline for destruction of the arsenals. The ICJ Advisory Opinion of 1996 came close to a non-use position also for nuclear weapons. The effects of nuclear arms are such that it is hard to imagine circumstances in which they could be used without colliding with humanitarian law. If the use is illegal, threats of use are illegal as well. A protocol banning the use of nuclear weapons, on the model of the Geneva Protocol, would convey the same message: the effects of nuclear weapons are such that no civilized state or sane leader should or would use them. As with the Geneva Protocol, it would in fact be a NFU agreement.

The best approach to NFU may be a gradual one in the form of

---

[9] So far, however, the US assurances have not been emulated by anybody else.

unilateral commitments as soon as more NWS are ready for it. There is much to build on: China adopted a NFU stance from the beginning; India emulated the US and added deterrence of chemical and biological weapons to its original NFU policy, but may be willing to go back on it; Russia and China have a bilateral NFU agreement; and the US says it will work to establish the conditions for NFU. A norm of no-first-use has emerged,[10] yet denial of it persists in the form of military contingency planning and threats of use. For the norm to get the strength of a taboo, a legal prohibition signed by all NWS is of essence.

The de-legitimation pathway

As with legal attempts to outlaw nuclear weapons use, public opinion mobilisation to delegitimise it is based, first and foremost, on humanitarian considerations. The humanitarians have some concrete successes to refer to, the landmines and cluster munitions conventions in particular. In the processes leading up to these agreements they built coalitions; they were goal-oriented; and they went for majority decisions rather than consensus texts on more modest measures. Arms controllers are known for the latter. The Geneva Conference on Disarmament is consensus stricken.

The International Campaign to Abolish Nuclear Weapons (ICAN) builds on this experience and on the lessons from chemical weapons disarmament. ICAN's main objective is to delegitimise nuclear weapons, outlaw their use and promote an international convention for disarmament to zero. There is much to speak for that campaign. However, the limitations should also be understood. Nuclear weapon issues are issues of high politics, i.e. they belong to the innermost sanctum of state interests. High politics – covering all matters that are vital to the survival of the state – has been present in all cultures and at all times, but the term was coined during the

---

[10] Nina Tannenwald argues that the norm of non-use is more than a prudential tradition: it has become a taboo. Traditions are not so strong that people accept them blindly. Taboos, on the other hand, imply an unthinking adherence to the norm. The taboo is a moral conviction: so far, there is no international legal instrument prohibiting the use of nuclear weapons, yet there is the strong impression that by using them, one would lose the high moral ground. Civilized nations and sane leaders do not use them first. Nina Tannenwald, *The Nuclear Taboo: The US and the Non-Use of Nuclear Weapons Since 1945*. Cambridge: Cambridge University Press, 2007.

Cold War. The advent of the atomic bomb made it clear what it was ultimately all about. The salience of landmines and cluster munitions is in a different category, way below that, accorded to nuclear arms.

Landmines and cluster munitions have, moreover, been in the hands of many governments while nuclear weapons have been acquired by a few. Majority conventions eliminating anti-personnel weapons therefore made sense: the inventories of many states are now being destroyed and more states may accede later on. A nuclear weapons convention, on the other hand, does not have the same prospect as long as the NWS oppose it. If initial support for a convention is limited to NNWS, no nuclear weapon would be dismantled as a consequence, and the convention would replicate the untenable NPT distinction between haves and have-nots.

The effects of nuclear weapons are also much different from those of chemical munitions; however often they are lumped into the same category of WMDs. On occasion, chemical agents have been used as weapons of terror, but they have not been effective means of war. Therefore, chemical weapons were never integrated into the military forces the way nuclear weapons are. The relevance for nuclear disarmament of the non-use/ elimination sequence of chemical weapons is limited also for that reason.

Nuclear history reconsidered: the revisionist pathway

In trying to show what nuclear weapons can do, the NWS have most probably inflated their utility. It has been customary to ascribe the Japanese surrender in 1945 to the bombing of Hiroshima and Nagasaki: it turns out that the Soviet declaration of war on Japan and its sweeping offensive in Manchuria were more important.[11] Shows of force and threats of nuclear weapon use may or may not have worked: in most cases the effects can neither be proved nor disproved. Realistic reviews of nuclear history in these respects, deleting the propagandistic arguments to uphold deterrence and justify investments in huge arsenals, can do much to reduce the attractiveness of nuclear arms.

The maze

Coming back to the present and to what has been called the maze, long lists of arms control and disarmament measures have been thoroughly examined and proposed over the years. Technically, virtually all stones may have been turned, most of them, many times over. Can arms control and disarmament measures that were conceived in the first nuclear age of the Cold War succeed under the political circumstances that underpin the second? To the extent that the classical propositions remain relevant, what would be the order of implementation?

Russia and the United States have conducted approximately 1000 nuclear weapon tests each: India 5. The advanced nuclear weapon states are increasingly sophisticated in simulating nuclear explosions: the latecomers do not have the same capabilities. Will the CTBT be accepted under such circumstances? Will it have to be supplemented by NWS commitments not to introduce new types of weapons, in the name of equity? Or should the sequencing be different, going for further substantial cuts first and trying to clinch a CTBT and an FMCT later? Art.VI of the NPT starts with "cessation of the nuclear arms race at an early date", which was always understood to be a reference to a CTBT and a FMCT (and to security assurances for NNWS), but there is nothing mandatory about the sequence in which the measures should be adopted. The proposal to make the INF Treaty universal cannot. In 1987, when the Treaty was concluded, few others had land-based missiles of intermediate range. Today, many states in Asia and elsewhere have made such vehicles their delivery systems of choice and would be much affected, while the US and Russia have a range of other delivery systems with their navies and air forces to rely upon. To Western voices arguing about nuclear disarmament, voices in the south and east say "go ahead, we will support you". But if the response is an arms control agenda that will constrain them while leaving the usual suspects largely off the hook, initiatives will quickly go sour. There is much to suggest that first priority should be given to deep cuts and doctrinal constraints, which does not preclude simultaneous attempts to clinch specific arms control measures.

Framing and timelines

How should it all be framed? How can disarmament in its two main

---

[11] Berry, Lewis, Pélopidas, Sokov and Wilson, *Delegitimizing Nuclear Weapons. Examining the validity of nuclear deterrence.* James Martin Center for Nonproliferation Studies, 2010.

dimensions – software and hardware – become a dependable prospect? If no fixed timeline can be agreed upon, can a dynamic disarmament process be ensured in other ways?

Similar to the integration theory, which distinguishes between integration as a process and integration as a state of affairs, disarmament may be viewed as a process where one move leads to the next, or it may be seen in a static perspective where measures are introduced without any particular promise or expectation of further steps.

The static perspective carries an immanent risk of reversal. When the continuation is uncertain, the action space for rearmament- – for qualitative improvements in particular – remains significant, thriving on the hedging argument. Single steps toward nuclear disarmament are, furthermore, unlikely to have much of an impact on governments contemplating to go nuclear. For instance, if the US and Russia were to reduce the number of deployed strategic nuclear weapons to 1,000 each, with no commitments to further reductions, while all NWS modernise their weapon systems, the non-proliferation impact would at best be uncertain and probably nil. As long as the continuation is open to doubt, states of proliferation concern would hardly be impressed. This is the situation today, Obama's disarmament overture notwithstanding. The Baruch plan of 1946, the McCloy-Zorin declaration of 1961 and the grand Reykjavik ambition of 1986 all failed, so a great many states are waiting to see what the fate of Obama's call will be.

This would be different if expectations were created that more would follow. Then, vested interests in the nuclear weapon sector would be constrained. In the NWS, the weight of R&D and procurement arguments would shift away from hedging and states of proliferation concern would be singled out as exceptions to a *trend* of improved compliance with regime obligations. It is always more difficult to act against an existing trend, especially if it enjoys broad support from both nuclear and non-nuclear weapon states. In the UN Security Council, decision-making in support of the trend would be easier.

The opposite of single steps in a static perspective is a convention with a timeline for nuclear disarmament to zero. The NPT is a roadmap to zero, but it is a rudimentary map; it says nothing about what kind of NWFW to go for; and the cracks in the non-proliferation regime that grew wide open in the beginning of this century, still need repair. The 2010 NPT Review Conference bought time for conflicting interests to be better managed, but achieved little more than that. At some stage, a more detailed, comprehensive agreement is therefore needed to guide the approach to abolition.

The Final Declaration of the 2010 NPT Review Conference noted, "the five-point proposal for nuclear disarmament of the Secretary-General of the United Nations, which proposes, *inter alia*, consideration of negotiations on a nuclear weapons convention or agreement on a framework of separate mutually reinforcing instruments, backed by a strong system of verification". The upside of the text is that the convention idea is mentioned; the downside, the convoluted and non-committal way in which it is composed. More than anything else, the P5 are opposed to any specific timeline for disarmament. Precisely because they have much power, they treasure the freedom to exercise it.

There is, furthermore, something simplistic about reducing the complexities of nuclear disarmament to a timeline. Who is to say when the problems posed by the missile defence and conventional prompt strike programs will be out of the way, if at all? When will Russia be ready to forego tactical nuclear weapons in defending the vast and thinly populated areas bordering China? Should a phased, time-bound disarmament plan fail the first test – in the Global Zero plan this is an agreement to go down to 1000 US and Russian weapons by 2013 – what about the rest? For some time ahead, the pertinent question is therefore, whether the disarmament process can be made dynamic and dependable without resorting to the calendar.

In the spirit of SC Resolution 1887, where the P5 declared themselves in favour of a world without nuclear weapons, it may be possible to generate explicit commitments from one step to the next: from New START to a follow-on agreement on deep cuts to further steps setting the stage for multilateral negotiations; from an FMCT to further cuts in fissile material stocks; from the steps taken by the US NPR to limit the role of nuclear weapons to a new SC Resolution on negative security assurances to an international convention on unqualified assurances to no-first-use doctrines; from procedural to material steps toward a NWFZ in the Middle East etc. – all the time, invoking the advantages of a NWFW, in support of the process. By dropping the timeline in favour of less ambitious provisions for progress, more states may be willing to entertain the convention idea. A convention without a timeline would be second best, but it may be preferable to having no convention at all.

Conclusion

For the time being, the challenge is to give momentum to nuclear disarmament without a convention and without a timeline, i.a. by forging commitments from one step to the next. A convention or a framework of mutually reinforcing instruments is desirable, the sooner the better. NWS participation should be sought from the beginning, not to replicate the NPT distinction between nuclear and non-nuclear weapon states. Should this depend on the timeline issue, a timeline had better wait. Beyond the deep cuts and NFU milestones, the path dependence of nuclear disarmament makes it hard to envisage how these and other issues would be phrased and resolved.

For all its weaknesses, the NPT and the regime that it harbours are a major achievement. The Treaty is resilient at that: in the beginning of this century, the grand bargain from the second half of the 1960s, on which it is based, came apart, yet it survived. Therefore, a nuclear weapon convention should not be pursued in order to replace it, but to supplement and supersede it. India seems well prepared for this. Since 1998, it has behaved more and more as if it was a member of the Treaty and it is increasingly integrated into the non-proliferation regime. At the same time, its ambitious disarmament policy is upheld and reinforced with a view to sustainable progress towards a NWFW.

All the time, two arguments carry particular weight. First, sixty years of no use do not guarantee another sixty years without the use of nuclear arms. On the contrary: there is much to suggest that the risk of nuclear weapon use is greater than before. The premium on abolition has therefore grown. For some proponents of a NWFW, this is hard-nosed realism. The four US horsemen were always known to be realists and so are many other statesmen that have joined them in the call for a NWFW. Other proponents stress that the threat of mass destruction is morally unacceptable and should be made unambiguously illegal. From both angles, MAD is an appropriate acronym for continued reliance on nuclear weapons and nuclear deterrence. The bottom line is that disarmament to zero must be pursued as a universal common good. If it is pursued and perceived in terms of unilateral advantage and national sacrifice, it will go nowhere.

Nuclear Base Camp: The Numbers Conundrum

T.P.Sreenivasan

Ever since J. Robert Oppenheimer invoked the Bhagavad Gita to create the mother of all metaphors, "the radiance of a thousand suns" and "the destroyer of worlds", nuclear weapons and disarmament efforts have given us many images and metaphors. But they were all images of mutually assured destruction and inevitability of a nuclear catastrophe. There was even a telling image of the world resting comfortably under the hood of a cobra. But more recently, despair has turned into hope with the metaphor of a mountain which, though distant and high, does hold the promise of a panoramic view of a nuclear weapon free and non-violent world, if the summit is reached. The world realises that the climb, up the mountain, will be slow and hazardous, but there appears to be a universal desire to make a determined effort.

The metaphor of the mountain has led to the image of a base camp, which is necessary to equip ourselves and to prepare for the climb. It is indeed a practical and necessary stage and translated into practical measures, it encourages all nations, whether they possess nuclear weapons or not, to build a staging ground. It means the establishment of intermediate goals towards disarmament on which there could be a consensus. The proponents of this concept have explained that the idea is to agree to proportional disarmament instead of smaller nuclear countries waiting till the others come down to their levels before they contemplate disarmament. They would like to craft a treaty, whereby countries, coming from different levels, could agree to work at reciprocal and proportional cuts, which would aim at all countries reaching the same lower number of weapons at a future date. William Perry characterises the base camp as a place that would be safer than the one in which the world is, today. It also serves as an organising principle to "lead, but hedge", in keeping with the US nuclear posture.

While the base camp concept is novel in the new context of optimism, it has been part of every plan that has been put forward in the past. Though the general and complete disarmament is the ultimate objective, giving priority to nuclear disarmament and that too through various intermediate stages is not very different from the base camp idea. The Rajiv Gandhi Action Plan of 1988 and the other practical steps put forward by various powers have contemplated intermediate stages of various descriptions. The proposal for a complete freeze was another logical step, which did not find acceptance with the nuclear weapon states. The proposed FMCT is another interim measure which is desirable and logical. Any step that reduces arsenals, strengthens non-proliferation and leads to elimination of nuclear weapons should be welcome.

It is not clear, however, whether the base camp concept can be approached on the basis of numbers. Such an approach has been adopted in the case of START, but the world is sceptical about the numbers involved in the negotiations as all categories of weapons are not included in the numbers game. Transparency is highly desirable, but often absent when it comes to counting weapons. Fixing agreed numbers to reach the base camp is likely to elude most. The idea of proportionate reduction in arsenals, regardless of the present size of the holdings will be anathema to those countries, which have only a minimum deterrent. India, for instance, has not revealed the number of weapons it considers necessary to have a credible minimum deterrent and the numbers are a matter of speculation. How would India participate in negotiations in reduction, without revealing the numbers?

A broader approach, which takes into account the new optimism, generated by President Obama's Prague speech, the sighting of the mountain, the encouraging signs at the latest NPT Review Conference and the Nuclear Security Summit, should move the disarmament effort forward.

India and the United States attempted precisely that at the summit level in their Joint Statement in 2011. The Prime Minister of India and the President of the United States had agreed to join in a "strong partnership to lead global efforts for non-proliferation and universal and non-discriminatory global disarmament." Further, "they affirmed the need for a meaningful dialogue among all states possessing nuclear weapons to build trust and confidence and for reducing the salience of nuclear weapons in international affairs and security doctrines." The key words here are "trust and confidence" and "reducing the salience of nuclear weapons" in strategies. This would be a very good start to the journey to the base camp and beyond, but not easy to do as it requires fundamental rethinking in many capitals of the world. As the Norwegian Foreign Minister observed, "Every small demonstration of our willingness to move forward towards abolition make many of the intermediate obstacles more surmountable."

The nuclear weapon states, sadly, still consider nuclear weapons important for their security and do not wish to consider a timeline for their elimination. The base camp, however, will not be meaningful unless there is a collective commitment to a multilateral framework for negotiations within a time frame. Neither the NPT nor the CTBT has succeeded in accomplishing this. The FMCT negotiations remain stalled. An alternate route will be, as India has suggested, working on a global non-first use agreement as the first step towards delegitimisation of nuclear weapons. Hesitation on de-legitimisation, on the ground that it will outlaw retaliation, seems unfounded as any use of the weapons will be unthinkable if there is de-legitimisation. A commitment to negotiating a Nuclear Weapons Convention may also be an appropriate element of the base camp.

Changing of postures, rather than agreeing on nuclear force sizes may be a practical approach to the base camp. In the case of the two countries, which possess 95% of the nuclear warheads, numbers are relevant to build mutual confidence, but for the others, the doctrinal commitment to nuclear weapons, regardless of numbers, is the greater threat. It is no great comfort for the world to know that the nuclear weapons can now destroy the world only a dozen times, not dozens of times.

The coming to force of the START has been universally welcomed. But further progress may be stalled on account of fears of China's growth. The focus is likely to shift to Asia, where the numbers game will be even more complex. In the Asian context, it will also be difficult to count the numbers considered necessary as minimum deterrent by different countries. Here again, a review of doctrines, rather than entering a debate on numbers, will have the desired impact.

The optimism that has entered the disarmament debate in recent years has not been fully justified by the latest signals from the major nuclear weapon states. The mountain and base camp images raise hope, but do not instill confidence. The urgency for nuclear disarmament, going beyond legal obligations has also been sidestepped in the process of setting up long term and intermediate stages. The time frame to reach global zero must be shorter if the world has to be safer.

Nuclear Doctrines and Military Realities

Bruno Tertrais

There are at least two different ways to describe the contemporary nuclear world. One can describe it as comprising a "Nuclear West" and a "Nuclear Rest". In the Nuclear West – the United States, the United Kingdom and France – nuclear weapons have clearly decreased in importance. But in the Nuclear Rest, they have become more important for security, status or regime preservation.

Another and probably a better way to describe the current nuclear world is to talk of an "Old Nuclear World", that of the Cold War, centred on the euro-Atlantic region, where nuclear arsenals are decreasing and a "New Nuclear World", that of Asia at large, where nuclear arsenals tend to increase or at least be developed. Any which way one looks at it, there is a good chance that the nuclear future will be written in Asia. One should also note the signing or coming into force of new treaties, establishing nuclear-weapon free zones; as a result, the nuclear world is now confined to the Northern Hemisphere; nuclear weapons are now legally banned from the largest part of the planet.

Many believe that one should now seek the abolition of nuclear weapons. Three different motivations are put forward. It is not like any of them is entirely persuasive. One is the longstanding idea that Nuclear Weapons States have a legal responsibility enshrined in Article 6 of the Non-proliferation Treaty to get rid of their nuclear arsenals. However, a careful reading of both the treaty and its negotiating record leads me to conclude that the legal obligations defined by the treaty are much more complex and subtle.[1] The International Court of Justice also gave an advisory opinion on this issue, but, in addition to the fact that it is not a legally-binding one, refrained from stating that this obligation existed separately from the broader obligation of Article 6.[2]

A second motivation is the alleged existence today of alternatives to nuclear weapons, such as modern conventional weaponry and missile defence. It is true that technology has advanced and matured, but nuclear weapons are still irreplaceable for the defence of vital interests, for three reasons.[3]

- First, because even modern conventional weapons do not have – or do not yet have – the same capabilities as nuclear weapons; for instance, they are unable to credibly put at risk hardened targets.

- Second, because it is only nuclear weapons, they can threaten to destroy any State as an organised entity in a matter of minutes. Of course, a long and sustained conventional bombing campaign could, in many scenarios, achieve the same result. But this would allow the adversary to adapt and adjust; such is the reason why conventional strategic city-bombing has rarely been efficient on its own. Moreover, in the information age, any massive bombing campaign would create intense political pressure on the government of the acting party – especially as casualties grow as they would, inevitably, for such an undertaking, which would look more like Dresden than Baghdad. And it would also leave time for the adversary to resort to non-conventional tactics such as terrorism.

- Third and most importantly, because of the scary and terrifying nature or nuclear weapons. As witnessed once again by the world reaction to the Fukushima accident, there is something irrational about the public perception of all things nuclear, which is at the

---

[1] Article 6 of the NPT states: "Each of the Parties to the Treaty undertakes to pursue negotiations in good faith on effective measures relating to cessation of the nuclear arms race at an early date and to nuclear disarmament, and on a treaty on general and complete disarmament under strict and effective international control."

[2] Para. 102 of the Advisory Opinion given by the ICJ in 1996, states: "There exists an obligation to pursue in good faith and bring to a conclusion negotiations leading to nuclear disarmament in all its aspects under strict and effective international control."

[3] For a more detailed analysis, see Bruno Tertrais, *In Defence of Deterrence*, Paris, Institut Français des Relations Internationales, September 2011.

root of deterrence. This is true even though the most important effects of nuclear weapons are blast and heat, not radiation.

For these reasons, it is easier to believe that it is very difficult to explain the historical anomaly that is the absence of any major power war since 1945, without nuclear weapons. Alternative explanations, from my point of view, are not satisfying.

What about missile defence? It is obviously an interesting complement to nuclear deterrence. Limited missile defence creates an additional layer of protection for cases in which nuclear deterrence does not apply – it is like having an airbag in addition to a safety belt, so to say – it increases the freedom of action of political authorities in times of crisis, and it raises the cost of aggression. But missile defence cannot threaten an adversary with unacceptable damage. And to rely exclusively on missile defense for the protection of vital interests would open the door to costly arms races. For those reasons, it is no substitute to nuclear deterrence.

A third motivation for disarmament is the increased – or at least the perceived increased – risk of nuclear proliferation and terrorism. However, there is a certain perplexity about this argument. As for proliferation, two decades of arms reductions have left the non-aligned countries unimpressed, new nuclear-capable countries unaffected and potential proliferators undaunted. As for terrorism, the connection fails except for the tautological proposition that if there were no nuclear weapons and fissile materials – well, there would not be any nuclear weapons and fissile materials.

Thus it is difficult to be persuaded by any of the three alleged reasons for going towards zero.[4] One could think of three different scenarios for analytical purposes, which could lead to zero. One could be political pressure for rapid disarmament after a major nuclear event, such as a regional nuclear war or an act of nuclear terrorism. Such is the reason why the preservation of the nuclear taboo is so important. Another scenario would be a progressive elimination of nuclear weapons after they become obsolete; as stated earlier, they will probably not become obsolete any time soon;

---

[4] For a more detailed analysis, see Bruno Tertrais, « The Illogic of Zero », The Washington Quarterly, vol. 33, n° 2, April 2010.

but one can envision the day where security and political conditions in the world may allow governments to embark on a process of progressive, coordinated reductions leading towards zero. The third and final scenario, which brings us back to the political realities of today, is that of a US-led initiative. This has been called the Prague Agenda.

Despite the best efforts of President Obama, of the so-called "Group of Four US Wise Men" and of their many friends around the world, it seems clear that the implementation of the Prague agenda has now been stalled. There are two main reasons for that. First, it is clear that despite the rhetoric of some, no nuclear-capable nation is ready to seriously consider the abolition of nuclear weapons. Second, the state of US domestic politics does not lend itself to major political initiatives in this domain. Many Republicans in Congress continue to show strong scepticism regarding abolition and it would not be a rational choice for the executive branch to spend too much political capital in this area. Especially given that the US public opinion does not really care anymore. The only nuclear issue that Americans really care about and which enjoys a bipartisan consensus is the reduction of the risk of nuclear terrorism. The New START and the Washington Summit on Nuclear Security were laudable initiatives, but they will have no impact on the chances of President Obama to be re-elected.

If one adds these two problems, one realises that the chances of a new arms control or disarmament treaty to come into force in the next five years are extraordinarily slim. Russia now insists that missile defence and conventional precision weapons be taken into account in the arms reduction process – which makes a new treaty almost impossible. Given the difficulties that even a modest agreement such as New START faced before Congress – remember that New START was not even a nuclear disarmament treaty in the strict sense of the term and would be more appropriately referred to as an arms control treaty – one should not anticipate that a more ambitious bilateral accord would do better.

On the question of "doctrinal obstacles", one is intrigued and a little bit perplexed by the subject given to tackle. Of course, it can be seen as to where this discussion may be leading: the generalisation of no-first-use postures would greatly simplify the abolition debate. But one cannot be sure that doctrines in themselves are an important obstacle to nuclear disarmament. Most of the time, though not always, doctrines are meant to respond to real or perceived specific security concerns and most of the time, are defined accordingly.

Most nuclear capable states have adapted to their nuclear doctrines in the past 20 years. It is not believe that any of them has "expanded" the scope of its doctrine – except perhaps Russia, which gave up no-first-use in 1993 and also India, which went in 2003 from unqualified no-first-use to qualified no-first-use. For most nuclear-capable countries, the threshold of nuclear use has always been a State attack against vital interests. The fact that the nature of the threat may change for some countries – in particular Western states – does not mean that the nuclear threshold had been "lowered".

Today China is the only nuclear-capable country which has an unqualified no-first-use doctrine. All others have declared, rightly or wrongly, that their nuclear weapons are also useful to deter non-nuclear threats. But even China occasionally hints at possible exceptions in its no-first-use doctrine, while some other States have introduced significant restrictions to their own doctrines. India has a policy of "not-quite-no-first-use", for instance and the United States has moved closer to a "sole purpose" doctrine. There is thus no simple distinction between "no-first-use countries" and others.

The generalisation of no-first-use doctrines would be an immense step towards nuclear disarmament. As my colleague of the Hudson Institute has written, it would make nuclear weapons "analytically isolated, self-supporting and self-justifying", which could lead us, according to him, to "fast-track nuclear disarmament".[5]

Doctrines do not always accurately reflect the state of the threat at a given moment in time. There is a certain amount of inertia and worse-case assumptions in nuclear policy-making. But most nuclear-capable states review on a regular basis, their security requirements. And many do not want to restrict the scope of their doctrines even when there is a relaxation of the threat, because it might be too costly politically to expand it again if a new threat was to reemerge.

Therefore, if one wants nuclear-capable countries to go in the direction of no-first-use, one has to deal with the underlying strategic rationales behind current nuclear doctrines. This means tackling two issues in particular. One is the continuing possession of chemical and especially biological weapons by several states, as well as active bio-warfare programs. Nuclear-capable countries will not adopt no-first-use posture without an assurance that no chemical or biological weapon threat may threaten their most vital interests. For those who believe that the chemical and biological weapons conventions could be models for the elimination of nuclear weapons, one needs to remind them, that for many countries, it was precisely the continuing existence of nuclear deterrence that made possible, their adhesion to those two conventions. The other task – an even more daunting one – is about eliminating the fear of a massive conventional attack in countries that feel that they are in a position of weakness, such as Russia and Pakistan. In this regard, one should remember that there is a clear connection in Article 6 of the Non-Proliferation Treaty, between nuclear disarmament and general and complete disarmament.[6] Conventional arms control and confidence-building measures can ease the pressure for such countries to have "early use" doctrines. But any real, long-term solution to this problem lies in the realm of politics and grand strategies, not of treaties.

The history of one particular region, the Middle East, bolsters the case for nuclear deterrence.[7] Egypt and Iraq were not ready to shy away from the use of chemical weapons, in Yemen and against Iran. But when they attacked Israel, they refrained from doing so. Regarding the 1973 war, it is also interesting to note that Cairo deliberately refrained from crossing the 1949 line, knowing that Israel was a nuclear power.

Moreover, experts think that there are fundamental problems with no-first-use.[8] Sometimes the adversary does not believe it, as was the case

---

[5] Chris Ford, *The Future of Nuclear Deterrence*, New Paradigms Forum, 24 March 2011.
[6] See above the text of Article 6.
[7] For a more detailed analysis, see Bruno Tertrais, *In Defence of Deterrence*, op. cit.

for the West regarding the Soviet Union, perhaps today also for the United States regarding China, or Pakistan regarding India. But if the adversary does believe it, then it knows that it can harm the opponent by whatever means and even threaten their most vital interests without incurring the risk of a nuclear response. One harbours the same doubts about the closely-related concept of "sole purpose", which differs from no-first-use in the fact that, strictly speaking, "sole purpose" does allow, at least theoretically, for the preemptive use of nuclear weapons against the adversary's nuclear forces.

A broader and perhaps deeper problem with no-first-use is that it greatly reduces the scope of nuclear deterrence and thus prevents it from playing a role across the whole spectrum of conflict. It makes the adversary able to calculate the risks inherent in an aggression. To proclaim a strict doctrine of no-first-use is to tell an adversary: "go ahead, whatever the means you will use against us, our retaliation will be strictly of a non-nuclear nature". In particular, it amounts to giving carte blanche to the adversary for using chemical weapons against the defender's troops, or biological weapons against its populations.

One other important value of nuclear weapons is that they project their shadow over the whole bilateral relationship between two countries. In Europe, in the Middle East, in South Asia and East Asia, the crises of the last 30 years happened under the nuclear shadow. They acted as a sort of brake against escalation. Incidentally, this is still true not only in Asia but even in Europe: without the presence of nuclear weapons; the Georgia crisis of 2008, for instance, might have unfolded differently.

If this sounds like a rather conservative discourse on nuclear deterrence, that is because it is one. I think that one will have to be very careful before jettisoning doctrines that have served well. No-first-use is an idea that time has not (yet) come, though it might be useful as a confidence-building measure between two countries. (In 1992, Russia and China declared that

---

[8] See Bruno Tertrais, « The Trouble With No-First-Use », Survival, vol. 51, n° 5, October-November 2009.

they would not be the first to use nuclear weapons against each other.)

However, most nuclear-armed nations could subscribe to the idea that the main or essential role of nuclear weapons in today's strategic context is to deter the use of nuclear weapons. It is interesting to note that the United States and the United Kingdom have adopted, in 2010, after reviewing their nuclear policies, doctrines that bring them very close to the one that India adopted in 2003.

Meanwhile, some other steps could be taken to anchor nuclear stability and security in the 21st century's nuclear world. The proposals for a new global nuclear regime can be summarised as "nuclear restraint". It also revolves around the notion of what is called "nuclear inclusiveness": it should not be limited to the five Nuclear Weapon States. One cannot reform the NPT: it is delusionary to expect that a consensus among all parties could ever be found for such a reform. A regime of nuclear restraint would be a set of principles to which all nuclear-capable nations could voluntarily and unilaterally subscribe, to be complemented by multilateral treaties, where applicable. It would include six distinct elements:

- First, doctrines should indicate clearly that nuclear weapons are not war-fighting weapons and that their use, which could only be of a "strategic" nature, would be considered only in the most extreme circumstances of self-defence, to defend vital interests;

- Second, planning should reject so-called "counterforce" options aimed at the destruction of the adversary's nuclear forces;

- Third, postures should discard any concept of launch-on-warning and the preemptive use of nuclear weapons; countries that possess land-based ballistic missiles should perhaps follow the Indian example of separating warheads and launchers.

- Fourth, there should be a complete cessation of both nuclear testing and the production of fissile material for weapons purposes; to that effect, taking into account the resistance of some nuclear-armed countries, one could think of declaring the provisional entry into force of the Comprehensive Test Ban Treaty; and consider negotiating a fissile material ban outside the Conference on Disarmament;

- Fifth, nuclear-armed countries should unilaterally adopt a modicum of transparency on their own nuclear forces in order to avoid States to make worst-case assumptions about their adversaries and thus fuel arms competitions;

- Sixth and finally, nuclear exports controls should be reinforced by more stringent standards, such as making the Additional Protocol of the International Atomic Energy Agency, a mandatory condition for any significant nuclear technology transfer.

Whether one likes it or not, one will have to live in a nuclear world for some time. The priority should be to manage this nuclear world as well as possible, for safety of the present as well as future generations.

Finally, on the question of elimination, it is well-known that security concerns are only one of the drivers of nuclear programs. Nuclear weapons are also political tools – for influence, prestige or international recognition. Removing this incentive for the possession of nuclear weapons will imply a serious reform of global governance. This should include a profound reform of the UN Security Council. It is time to break for good, the symbolic convergence that exists with being a victor of the Second World War, a legitimate possessor of nuclear weapons and a permanent member of the Security Council. In particular, a reform of the UN Security Council, which would give to several non-nuclear States the same rights and privileges as the Five, could be a crucial non-proliferation measure. Ultimately, the reform of the nuclear order cannot be separated from the reform of the global political order.

Role of Nuclear Weapons in NATO's Strategic Concept

Jacek Bylica[1]

This essay attempts to deal with NATO-India dialogue in general and in the nuclear field in particular, focussing on the results of the Lisbon Summit in November 2011, but more importantly, on what has been happening in NATO since and what some of the future relevant plans are. This includes the process initiated after Lisbon, under the name of the Deterrence and Defence Posture Review. There is also an attempt to outline some proposals under discussion in the Alliance, as far as they are relevant to the future of nuclear weapons and in particular, the tactical nuclear weapons.

NATO-India dialogue and WMD non-proliferation

One important part of NATO's transformation in recent years has been the development of closer relations with countries from across the globe. NATO Secretary General, Anders Fogh Rasmussen has been repeatedly arguing for developing closer relations with all major global players, including India and China.

Only a few years ago, any mentioning of India and China as potential NATO partners would have led to raised eyebrows not only in Delhi and Beijing, but also in many NATO member countries. Not any more. The suggestion to use NATO as a forum for consultation and cooperation is very pragmatic: in an age that is increasingly shaped by the forces of globalisation, managing common security challenges requires a much tighter

[1] Mr. Jacek Bylica is the Head of WMD Non-Proliferation Centre (WMDC) at NATO since 2008. Prior to joining NATO's International Staff, from 2004 to 2008, he was Poland's Ambassador to Vienna-based international organisations and control regimes, including the IAEA and NSG. These seminar remarks do not necessarily reflect NATO official positions.

network among the key players.

Still, many Indian analysts harbour doubts about the possible implications for their country's international position if it should develop closer ties with NATO. But the international stature of countries as diverse as Russia, China, Japan, Egypt or Australia has not suffered from their cooperation with NATO. Hence, India will not need to compromise the fundamental tenets of its foreign and security policy. As Switzerland's long-standing cooperation with NATO should demonstrate even to the most ardent sceptics, neither non-alignment nor neutrality need to prevent a country from cooperating with NATO.

For many Indian observers, the suggestion of dealing with NATO on WMD non-proliferation issues will appear far-fetched. After all, when it comes to the most frequently discussed type of WMD, namely nuclear weapons, the respective characteristics of India and NATO could hardly be more different:

On the one hand, there is India, a nation-state with a non-aligned tradition, situated in a volatile security environment that includes failing states in its immediate neighbourhood and complex relations with two other nuclear weapons states, namely Pakistan and China. Accordingly, India's nuclear deterrent serves the sole purpose of defending the nation – its nuclear deterrence is thus seen as an entirely national issue. Moreover, India is not a member of the NPT – a fact that sets it apart from almost all other nations, given that the NPT has meanwhile become one of the most universal international agreements.

On the other hand, there is NATO, an alliance of meanwhile 28 nation states, among them three Nuclear Weapons States. Since the end of the Cold War, NATO's immediate neighbourhood has become much less volatile; it is in no way comparable to India's. In NATO, nuclear deterrence is not just a means to protect the national territory of the three NWS, but also serves as protection for the Alliance as a whole. To this end, the United States offers "extended deterrence" commitments to its Allies – commitments that are implemented in NATO through an elaborate network of nuclear sharing and consultation arrangements. All NATO members are also members of the NPT and they subscribe to the principle of universal adherence to this Treaty.

According to key NATO documents, the members of the Alliance consider two kinds of threats to constitute their major security challenges over the next 10 to 15 years. One is terrorism; the other is the proliferation of WMD. Accordingly, NATO has developed a comprehensive policy on WMD, a policy that includes the analysis of WMD threats, intelligence sharing, developing means to detect and trace back attacks, developing means to deter WMD attacks and to deal with their consequences if they should occur and various arms control and non-proliferation measures. The policy also includes closer cooperation with other international institutions. And it includes cooperation with partner countries.

Nuclear weapons in the documents of the Lisbon Summit

The Lisbon Summit of the North Atlantic Treaty Organisation (19-20 November 2010) adopted a number of decisions of strategic importance for the security of the trans-Atlantic community. Among them, the greatest interest was attracted by the New Strategic Concept for the Defence and Security of the Members of the North Atlantic Treaty Organisation "Active Engagement, Modern Defence".

In addition to the new Strategic Concept, the Lisbon Summit also adopted other documents important for understanding the Alliance's new political philosophy and how it will be brought into practice. These documents specify NATO's position on all key security and defence issues, and especially prospects for the Alliance's engagement in Afghanistan, relations with Russia, support for arms control, disarmament and non-proliferation and other detailed issues.

This chapter concentrates on the aspects relevant to nuclear weapons and the future of disarmament.

First of all, Heads of State and Government of NATO Countries, assembled at the Summit in Lisbon, reaffirmed their assessment that the proliferation of nuclear weapons and other weapons of mass destruction and their means of delivery, threatens incalculable consequences for global stability and prosperity. They assess and this is reflected in the New Strategic Concept, that during the next decade, proliferation will be most acute in some of the world's most volatile regions. These regions are not named in the Concept.

As a direct result of this threat assessment, they decided to commit NATO, inter alia, to:

[1] continue to play part in reinforcing arms control and in promoting disarmament of both conventional weapons and WMD, as well as non-proliferation efforts;

[2] develop the capability to defend populations and territories against ballistic missile attack, while actively seeking cooperation on missile defence with Russia and other Euro-Atlantic partners;

[3] further develop NATO's capacity to defend against the threat of chemical, biological, radiological and nuclear weapons of mass destruction.

The Strategic Concept commits the Alliance to a policy of deterrence based on an appropriate mix of nuclear and conventional forces which remains a core element of the Alliance's overall strategy. The Lisbon Summit Declaration also states that NATO will maintain an appropriate mix of conventional, nuclear and missile defence capabilities.

The Strategic Concept clearly reconfirms that NATO will remain a nuclear Alliance as long as nuclear weapons exist, notwithstanding the fact that the circumstances in which any use of nuclear weapons might have to be contemplated are extremely remote. It stresses the role of US, UK and French strategic nuclear forces in providing NATO with a supreme guarantee of security. Moreover, the Strategic Concept underlines the importance of the broadest possible participation in collective defence planning in nuclear roles, in peacetime basing and in command-and-control arrangements.

NATO's nuclear weapons no longer target any country. NATO does not have a no-first use policy, neither does it have a first use policy. The weapons are to ensure uncertainty in the mind of any agressor about the nature of Allies' response to military aggression.

At the same time, the Strategic Concept and the Lisbon Summit Declaration commit the Alliance to create the conditions for a world without nuclear weapons, for future reductions in NATO's nuclear stockpile and for further reducing the salience of nuclear weapons in its deterrence and defence posture. This means that the Alliance has in fact not only embraced the long term vision of a nuclear-free world, but is in fact ready to make practical contributions, by working to create appropriate conditions. The Summit Declaration further commits NATO to seek universal adherence to the NPT and full compliance with its obligations. The Alliance is also committed to conventional arms control regime in Europe on the basis of reciprocity, transparency and host nation consent.

The Lisbon Declaration tasked the North Atlantic council to continue to review NATO's overall posture in deterring and defending against the full range of threats to the Alliance, taking into account changes in the evolving security environment.

From Lisbon to Chicago: a Deterrence and Defence Posture Review

The Deterrence and Defence Posture Review (DDPR) will be a comprehensive review of the capabilities and instruments that NATO will require to uphold effective deterrence and secure defence in the security environment of the 21st century. These capabilities and instruments will include nuclear weapons and posture, missile defence, the role of conventional forces in enhancing Allied security and other means of strategic deterrence and defence, particularly in coping with emerging security challenges such as proliferation of WMD and ballistic missiles, cyber attacks, terrorism, threats to critical infrastructure and supply routes, as well as energy security. NATO's nuclear posture review will only apply to nuclear weapons assigned to NATO by two Allies: US and UK.

DDPR will also examine the contribution of NATO's activities in the areas of crisis management, cooperative security, partnerships, as well as arms control, disarmament and non-proliferation – to an overall Alliance strategy of collective defence and enhancing security and stability beyond the Alliance's borders.

Based on the Terms of Reference which were agreed on by NATO Defence Ministers in March 2011, DDPR will be conducted in two phases:

An exploratory thematic phase, which will be completed in the Summer or early Autumn of this year; and a drafting and negotiating phase to prepare a final document, which will be completed in time for the NATO Summit, tentatively planned for May 2012 in Chicago.

The North Atlantic Council (the Ambassadors) will retain overall responsibility for the process, seeking advice and inputs from other bodies within NATO as it decides. During Phase 1 (the exploratory phase) of the DDPR, which began in early May, the NAC will be considering the following broad topics which have been approved by NATO Foreign Ministers in a Work Plan.

[1] What are the threats, challenges and opportunities in today's dynamic international security environment?

In this context, Allies will analyse how the security environment has changed, or is likely to change, in ways that could impact NATO's deterrence and defence postures and capabilities. To the extent possible, they will review the defence plans and capabilities of countries outside the Alliance which could affect NATO, as well as assess the threat posed by transnational challenges such as terrorism, cyber attacks or the possible disruption of transport and transit routes.

[2] What are the requirements for NATO's deterrence and defence?

In this context, Allies will examine the full range of NATO's strategic capabilities, including the Alliance's nuclear posture and missile defence, as well as other means of deterrence and defence, to ensure that it can continue to uphold the security for all. They will obviously take into account the Allies' arms control, disarmament and non-proliferation efforts.

[3] What is the appropriate mix of capabilities to meet NATO's requirements?

In this context, Allies will examine how NATO's strategic capabilities (nuclear, conventional, missile defence) inter-relate and complement each other. They will discuss the relative contribution of these core capabilities to deterrence and defence in the new environment and whether any modifications to this mix are required in the future. Finally, Allies will evaluate how arms control negotiations, whether bilateral or multilateral, could evolve in the future and how they could affect NATO's posture.

In Phase 2 (drafting and negotiating phase), the NAC will provide guidance on the structure and contents of the Review document and seek input and advice from appropriate committees on elements of it as considered appropriate.

The NAC will also seek outside expertise and views on these various topics. This will take the form of various seminars and informal meetings. Both Foreign and Defence Ministers will be closely involved in the DDPR. In particular, following the exploratory phase, Ministers will provide specific guidance for the drafting of DDPR during their meetings in the Autumn of 2011.

As mentioned before, currently NATO's aim is to finalise the DDPR and agree to it by the time of the next Summit, planned to be held in the US, in the Spring of 2011. Needless to say, as all decisions in NATO, also this one will be taken by consensus.

Let me stress that the results of the Posture Review are not preordained. The current Strategic Concept states that NATO will remain a nuclear Alliance as long as nuclear weapons exist, but the type and numbers of these weapons, as well as NATO's declaratory policy with respect to NW will be addressed as part of the Review process.

Finally, the future progress of various arms control negotiations, both bilateral and multilateral, can have an important influence on the Posture Review. NATO supports the US intention to engage Russia in negotiations on nuclear weapons in Europe and the issue of increasing the transparency on tactical nuclear weapons has been raised by a number of countries, but prospects for progress remain yet unclear. But what is clear is that also in this way, countries from outside of the Alliance could have an impact on the results of NATO's Deterrence and Defence Posture Review.

Conclusion

NATO remains a nuclear Alliance committed to a policy of deterrence. It has declared that it will remain a nuclear alliance as long as nuclear weapons exist. At the same time, NATO supports international arms control, disarmament and non-proliferation efforts and has committed to create the conditions for a world without nuclear weapons, for future further reductions in NATO's nuclear stockpile and for further reducing the salience of nuclear weapons in its deterrence and defence posture. What's more, NATO has instituted a process of reviewing its defence and deterrence posture, with results to be visible by the time of the next NATO Summit, tentatively planned for May 2012. Two issues on which discussion is particularly active are the future of tactical nuclear weapons stationed in Europe and the role of missile defence capabilities as they relate to deterrence. On both issues, dialogue and interaction with the Russian Federation will be of paramount importance.

Nuclear Doctrines and Military Realities

Prakash Menon

Introduction

Political and Strategic behaviour of nation states are rooted in belief systems harboured by the ruling elite. Belief systems provide the raw material that constructs what is perceived as the existential political reality which acts as the prism that shapes behaviour. This, in turn, predominantly influences the form and content of a nation state's interactions with the international system and its domestic constituencies. For most of the nuclear weapon states, military inputs have exercised considerable influence in shaping the form and content of nuclear doctrines. Military inputs understandably base their prescriptions on worst case scenarios and the constant need to hedge against the unknown. Constructed or assumed military realities in the nuclear realm tend to treat nuclear weapons as another type of weapons albeit with a much higher grade of destructive ability. This is despite the fact that nuclear use between nuclear weapon states creates the conundrum of severing the relationship between use of force and achievement of political objectives.

Doctrines of Nuclear Weapon States however served to communicate the political message as to what a particular state wished to achieve with nuclear weapons and how it proposes to do so. Most nations have publicised nuclear doctrines, while some have preferred to convey their beliefs through periodic policy statements. In terms of audience, doctrines address both domestic and international constituencies. Nuclear doctrines also fashion the desire of non-nuclear-weapon states to acquire or not to acquire nuclear weapons. Nuclear doctrines are expected to be dynamic as they should adjust to the perceived changes in the political landscape. This however, is not quite true as the weight of habit derived from the past, coupled with the military proclivity for worst case scenarios and the felt need to minimise damage and destruction often tends to create inertia for maintaining the status quo. The resistance to change of doctrines despite change in the political landscape is thus primarily derived from military bureaucracies within the nuclear weapon states. The Cold War legacy and the extant US and Russia nuclear disarmament attempts are illustrative.

Cold War Legacy

The Cold War was over nearly two decades ago. Yet the USA and Russia continue to maintain weapons on hair trigger alert even though they are now targeted by mutual agreement towards the "open oceans". Over 2000 of the United States' and Russian weapons remain on a dangerously high alert warning in the event of a perceived attack, within a decision window for each President of four to eight minutes. What possible justification can there be for such a posture when political realities do not require such strategic behaviour? The answer perhaps lies in the emotion of fear on which the entire edifice of deterrence and especially nuclear deterrence is founded. The military, charged with 'working the system', tries to seek as many options as possible to make the best out of what is fundamentally a situation fraught with great risk and uncertainty. Numbers are believed to matter and keeping weapons to be able to react at the shortest notice, takes care, at least to some extent, of the element of surprise, especially in case of the "bolt from the blue" attacks.

The United States' NPR considered the possibility of reducing alert rates for ICBMs and at-sea rates of SSBNs and concluded that such steps could reduce crisis stability by giving an adversary the incentive to attack before "re-alerting" was complete. The urge to hedge against the unknown, creates the forces that impede reduction of risks posed by nuclear weapons. It is a thought process that is primarily military driven, even when it increases the chances of inadvertent and accidental nuclear exchange. Apparently the military succeeds in convincing the politicians that the risk is tolerable.

But what has happened in the last few years is that the practitioners of the Cold War nuclear standoff are now saying in unison that the risks are not worth taking and there is a dire need to reduce the salience of nuclear weapons in pursuit of a vision for global zero.

In fact, in June 1988, India's Prime Minister Rajiv Gandhi promoted an Action Plan at the United Nations for phased nuclear disarmament and in his fervent plea had said that "this madness must stop". The call was welcomed by the Soviet Union and rejected by the United States. In recent times, the same call is getting strident and comes from a substantial portion of the international spectrum, with the 2007 Wall Street Journal article of Kissinger, Schultz, Perry and Nunn, the Gareth Evans and Yoriko Kawaguchi report, President Obama's 2009 Prague speech etc. *inter alia* setting the tone of the discourse.

Even as world leaders call for nuclear disarmament, the uncertainty of future political relations applies brakes to change. The present generation of leaders now led by President Obama has supported the vision of Global Zero. The ratification of the new START Treaty by the USA and Russia is a positive step in the long road to Global Zero. For all the advances achieved by these agreements and some additional unilateral decision-making, the two states' total arsenal of useable warheads still remains huge: some 9,400 for the U.S. and 13,000 for Russia. The remaining nuclear powers have amongst them about 1000 weapons. On the best available current estimates (some but not all figures are on the public record) these numbers can be sub-divided as follows[1]:

For the U.S. 9400 nuclear warheads, of which:

- some 2200 are operationally-deployed strategic warheads.

- some 500 are operationally-deployed "sub-strategic" warheads.

- around 2500 warheads are in reserve (of which some 500 are "sub-strategic").

- around 4200 are awaiting dismantlement.

---

[1] Gareth Evans & Yoriko Kawaguchi, Eliminating Nuclear Threats, Report of the International Commission on Nuclear Proliferation and Disarmament, WWW.ICNND.ORG

For Russia, 13000 nuclear warheads, of which:

- close to 2800 are operationally-deployed strategic warheads

- roughly 2000 are operationally-deployed "sub-strategic" warheads

- an estimated 8150 warheads are in reserve or awaiting dismantlement (of which some 3400 are "sub-strategic")

The new START agreement, signed in 2009 and ratified in 2011, commits both states to a total of 1550 accountable strategic warheads, 700 deployed strategic delivery vehicles and 800 deployed and non-deployed strategic launchers. A huge exercise remains to bring down overall numbers of warheads – including sub-strategic weapons and those in reserve and awaiting dismantlement. But the road ahead is mined with a plethora of issues that the nuclear domain poses.

Nuclear Domain and Geopolitics

The nuclear domain, in its entirety, rests on geopolitical space. Nuclear weapons are more so about geopolitics. A nation state is influenced by a host of factors in its orientation and world view; amongst the ones that are real and non negotiable are the construct of its geography and history. Geography provides the state with its neighbours, resources and the compelling dynamics of the external connect. It also defines the parameters of economy, socio-cultural connects, interests and ambitions and the complete range of leverages related to these. History casts the approach of the leadership and people as also creates or subsumes issues of external relationship. Globally and regionally, countries remain in pursuit of a status in which stakes of all those concerned acquire a competitive mode. A nuclear leverage in this paradigm of strategic competition is believed to be an instrument of power where objectives could be met without causing, it is hoped, unmanageable and protracted tension. Strategies and doctrines are woven around core interests in a constant bid to strengthen a country's leverage in altering or retaining the status quo. The strategies and doctrines are founded on fear, created by an existential threat, coupled with uncertainty; it also relies, for success, on the manipulation of risk by leaders who are expected to be rational under conditions when fear is the preponderant emotion.

Dangers of Risk Manipulation

In times of crisis, military and political signals are easily misunderstood. Both military and political leaders realised during the Cold War, that once nuclear weapons were used, it would be difficult to prevent the unleashing of more nuclear weapons because each side would attempt to minimise damage to it by trying to neutralise the nuclear capability of the other. It was therefore impossible to devise a nuclear strategy that did not have a significant risk of arriving at the outcome it was meant to avoid. Theories of intra war deterrence and nuclear war fighting were mostly military fictions that sought to strengthen deterrence credibility, but once deterrence was broken, its consequences were pregnant with horrendous possibilities. So, the need for exercising caution when nuclear weapons were involved has been the legacy of the Cold War experience. Rationally, any attempt at trying to gain the upper hand while manipulating nuclear risks needs to be eschewed. Unfortunately, most NWS, except perhaps India and China have not reflected on this essential learning in their nuclear doctrines. Most continue to threaten the use of nuclear weapons under certain conditions even against conventional threats and these are reflected in their nuclear doctrines.

Nuclear Doctrines

United States. US nuclear policy objectives now encircle the need to prevent nuclear proliferation and nuclear terrorism; strengthen regional deterrence to tackle regional seekers of nuclear weapons; maintain strategic deterrence with reduced relevance/ numbers of US nuclear weapons. The US still retains the relevance of nuclear weapons as a means of deterring WMD attack also for its allies[2]. The non-use of nuclear weapons excludes states violating their obligations under the NPT. The Quadrennial Defence Review and Ballistic Missile Defence Review echo the requirement to strengthen deterrence while reducing the role of nuclear weapons, including investments in missile defences, counter-WMD capabilities and other conventional military capabilities. The adoption, by the US, of a universal

---

[2] Nuclear Posture Review Report, April 2010, Department of Defence -United States of America, www.defense.gov/npr/docs/2010

policy that the "sole purpose" of U.S. nuclear weapons is to deter nuclear attack on the United States and its allies and partners is yet to be fructified.

Russia. The Russian Military Doctrine of 05 February 2010 defines its right to use nuclear weapons. Thus: "the Russian Federation retains the right to use nuclear weapons in response to an attack against itself or its allies with the use of nuclear and other weapons of mass destruction and in case of aggression against the Russian Federation, with use of conventional weapons when the very existence of the state is threatened."[3] For deterring and preventing armed conflicts, thus, Russia would require "maintaining sufficient level of strategic stability and nuclear deterrence capability".

The change is in comparison to the 2000 Military Doctrine of the Russian Federation that spoke of the right to use nuclear weapons in "situations critical to the national security of the Russian Federation". The change in the wording of the 2010 Military Doctrine, regarding the condition for using nuclear weapons, is perhaps insignificant in form but very important in terms of the implication in that it raises the threshold of use of nuclear weapons[4]. However, there is definitely a lack of clarity on threats to "the very existence of the nation", that is, Russia. The May 2009 National Security Strategy of the Russian Federation, through 2020, lists threats from "the policies of a number of leading foreign states, directed at achieving predominant superiority in the military sphere, primarily in terms of strategic nuclear forces, by developing high-precision, informational and other advanced means of warfare, strategic non-nuclear arms, as well as by unilaterally creating a global missile defence system and militarising space"[5]. For Russians, the threat emanates not from any large-scale conventional/ nuclear war but in the creation and deployment of strategic missile defences, undermining the balance of powers; militarisation of outer space;

---

[3] Military Doctrine of the Russian Federation, 5 Feb 2010, http:news.kremlin.ru/ref_notes/ 461

[4] Alexei Arbatov, Vladmir Dworkin and Sergey Oznobishchev, " Contemporary Nuclear Doctrines", Publication of Joint Threat Initiative (NTI) AND Institute of World Economy and International Relations (IMEMO) of the Russian Academy of Sciences project conference (Moscow 2010)

[5] National Security Strategy of the Russian Federation through to 2020, 13 May 2009. http:/ /www.president.kremlin.ru/ref.notes/424

deployment of strategic conventional high-precision weapons, proliferation of weapons of mass destruction/missiles and missile technologies; and an increase in the number of nuclear-weapons states.

China. The Chinese have remained steadfast in declaration of their adherence to NFU. Its arsenal and policies have remained opaque which is destabilising and increases fears of their actual intentions. However, the retaliatory strength and capability of China especially in the event of a disarming nuclear attack by the United States or Russia is in question. It is also not far from surmise that Chinese nuclear forces modernisation programs will increase its survivable retaliation capability and the fast paced developments in ASBM, ALCM and space based programs could be seen in this light. China can therefore be expected to oppose any proposal that calls for a freeze at present levels.

France. Nuclear deterrence for France is the means for its country's independent stance in the international community of nuclear powers as also a guarantor of security. It is the means to protect its vital interests (integrity of its territory, the safety of its people and sovereignty) and an attack on these would entail unacceptable damage "wherever it may come from and in whatever shape or form."[6] France has maintained its reservations against a No First Use. It does not favour a war fighting strategy and has fixed a minimum yield for the new weapons. A nuclear response is a declared possibility only in "extreme circumstances of self defence."[7] France, it needs note, is the one country that developed, deployed and then decided to do away with ground launched ballistic missiles, dismantled nuclear test sites and fissile material production facilities and supports a zero test – whatever the yield. France's main worries include a nuclear Middle East at some near date as also of nuclear-armed states in North Africa. An ICBM capability with North Korea is an additive of its Asian concerns apart from the growing powers of China. France has a small but modern force maintaining that the level of its capability and numbers in arsenal are

---

[6] French White Paper on Defence and National Security, 2008 www. livreblancdefenseetsecurite. gouv.fr

[7] Bruno Tertrais, "French Perspectives on Nuclear Weapons and Disarmament", in Blencham ed, *Unblocking the road to Zero: Perspectives of Advanced Nuclear Nations* (February 2009).

independent of what the other nuclear states have/need.

United Kingdom [8]. British nuclear capability seems primarily focussed on ballistic missile carrying submarines. Interestingly, there is no real rationale for British nuclear forces except as an additive to the Western alliance of nuclear haves and possibly as a measure of response to a chemical or biological warfare. UK seems far from being threatened by non-nuclear contingencies or nuclear conflicts per se. Britain has never made any claims to military value of its nuclear arsenal neither have they avowed nationalistic or prestige oriented rationale. Their nuclear policy has been in sync with the nuclear allies over the years with an element of independent standing in the community of nuclear haves. Notable is the fact that the risk of proliferation in the third world has been used as a reason for British nuclear deterrent. It is not clear whether UK would be an able provider of support to its allies in this part of the world against any nuclear threat though they could use deterrence doctrines against any threats of use of WMD from these regions. There remains an ambiguity regarding the weightage of nuclear weapons against biological and chemical weapons threats. The December 2006 Defence White Paper refers to the presence of nuclear arsenals, nuclear proliferation, nuclear terrorism etc. as some of the reasons for a minimum nuclear deterrent.

NATO. NATO's 2010 Strategic Concept [9] refers to the "dramatic reduction" in the number of nuclear weapons stationed in Europe, post Cold War and the lowered "reliance on nuclear weapons in NATO strategy". However the Concept maintains that NATO will remain a nuclear Alliance in the light of the "evolving set of challenges to the security of NATO and as long as there are nuclear weapons in the world". While there is an increasing resistance to tactical nuclear weapons on European soil, the former Warsaw countries who are now part of the European alliance prefer that these weapons remain. The report of the Group of Experts, headed by Dr. Madeleine Albright, outlines major ideas of the future Strategic Concept

---

[8] Lawrence Freedman, British Perspectives on Nuclear Weapons and Nuclear Disarmament", in Blencham ed , *Unblocking the road to Zero: Perspectives of Advanced Nuclear Nations* (February 2009).

[9] The Alliance's Strategic Concept. 24 April 1999 http://www.nato.int/cps/en/natolive/official_texts_27433.htm

("NATO 2020"), which states that "because Russia's future policies toward NATO remain difficult to predict, the Allies must pursue the goal of cooperation while also guarding against the possibility that Russia could decide to move in a more adversarial direction".[10] This reasoning has prompted retention of the role of nuclear weapons in the November 2010 Strategic Concept of NATO.

Pakistan. Pakistan has no formal nuclear doctrine and has sought to convey its purposes and policies through public statements. Its nuclear weapons are singularly oriented towards India. Minimum nuclear deterrence with first use is claimed by Pakistani political and military leaders to be one of the fundamental features of Pakistan's nuclear doctrine.[11] Pakistan rejected India's proposal for a joint no-first use pledge in the immediate aftermath of May 1998 nuclear tests as "unacceptable." According to General Khalid Kidwai, Pakistan would use nuclear weapons in the event: India attacks Pakistan and conquers a large part of its territory; destroys a large section of its land and air forces; does an economic strangulation of Pakistan; pushes Pakistan into political destabilisation or creates large-scale internal subversion[12]. It is obvious that Pakistan's strategy is based on looking ferocious while actually being weak. However their past paced nuclear developments and internal crises are matters worrisome to the global community. Its contemporary internal situation has increased the possibility of nuclear material and weapons falling into the hands of jihadis. An added danger is that Pakistan's nuclear weapons are controlled by its military who are naturally inclined to risk manipulation and being rash.

India. India's nuclear doctrine is based on No First Use, Minimum deterrence and Civilian Control. India's Nuclear Policy Seeks Deterrence only at the Grand Strategic Levels. India's leaders mainly consider nuclear weapons a political instrument for employment at the level of grand strategy, not as a winning tool for military operations. The concept of "what wins,

---

[10] NATO 2020: Assured Security. Dynamic Engagement, Analysis and Recommendations of the Group of Experts on a New Strategic Concept for NATO. 17 May, 2010 (http://www.nato.int/cps/en/natolive/official_texts_63654.htm).

[11] Smriti Pattanaik, "Pakistan's Nuclear Strategy", Strategic Analysis, Vol 27, No 1, Jan –Mar 2003, www.idsa.in/system/files/strategicanalysis.smruti.0303.pdf

[12] Amir Mir, "The Man who secures Pak Nukes", Daily News and Analysis, 23 November 2007.

deters" does not guide India's nuclear thinking. We have not stratified nuclear operations into strategic, operational, or tactical levels. A nuclear strike against Indian territory or its assets, whether with high or low-yield warheads, causing either great or small losses is seen as an attack that invokes its counterattack. Other global practices, by comparison, incorporate nuclear war fighting into strategic, operational and tactical operations. India has also kept the option open for retaliating with nuclear weapons against Biological and Chemical attacks.

Core Deterrence

One of the major factors that resist change is the inability of nuclear powers to jettison the belief that nuclear weapons have roles beyond the core deterrence role of deterring nuclear weapons. The point at issue is that there is a need to realise and accept that roles beyond the core deterrence role are fraught with danger and carry substantial risk of spilling across the nuclear threshold. But the belief is difficult to jettison if the perceived geopolitical interests demand extension of the nuclear role. Weakening of Russia's conventional capability resulted in expanding the role of Russia's nuclear weapons in the period after the demise of the Soviet Union. The need to extend deterrence to its NATO allies, South Korea, Japan and the conventional superiority of Russia keeps the door open in the nuclear doctrines of the United States and NATO for use of nuclear weapons against conventional threat. China's military threat, even if conventional, against Taiwan, is sought to be deterred by the United States through nuclear threats. Pakistan cites its conventional weakness with India to threaten use of nuclear weapons against Indian conventional threats.

All countries have stated that nuclear retaliation is a possibility if attacked by biological or chemical weapons. There is however room for argument that this need not be the case. Firstly, biological and chemical weapons have to be used on a very large scale to create the type and speed of devastation that the nuclear weapons are capable of which makes their utility questionable. Secondly, though biological weapons in sufficient quantity can be potentially devastating, it is very difficult to preserve and transport, thus making it difficult for use by non-state actors. Thirdly, chemical weapons, though the easiest to manufacture, not only require massive quantities but is also difficult to control in terms of direction, due to uncertain winds. Fourthly, a doctrinal threat to use nuclear weapons against biological and chemical weapon use may invite a low impact use and test the credibility of the threat. In any case, since most countries have signed the Chemical and Biological weapons Convention, it's use by a state who is signatory can justify the use of nuclear weapons using the principle of belligerent reprisal[13].

So, it is obvious that the impact of global and regional geopolitics cannot easily be overcome even if it is realised and believed that at the root, it is a dangerous game that is better avoided. The danger can be minimised if Nuclear Weapon States accept that use of force to change the status quo between nuclear powers is fraught with uncertainties that are better left untested. Therefore change must be sought through other means than nuclear weapons. The moot question is whether such a notion is acceptable to the Nuclear Weapon States in the background of the extant state of international relations.

Contemporary World Politics

International Relations in the global system is witness to two competing dynamics are at work. On the one hand, most countries, including India, seem to extol the virtues of economic interdependence; they are enhancing their power, not through isolation but by creating webs of interdependence: financial, trade and economic. In this scenario, international relations appear to be in a peaceful win – win situation. In this liberal internationalist vision, countries that are interdependent are likely to work together to secure a stable international order, old territorial rivalries are passé and a web of institutional affiliations in the international system is likely to triumph over standard nationalist ambitions. On the other hand, there is a version of the world where traditional great power rivalry continues to be the foundation around which international discourse is organised: in this view, power is a zero sum game, nationalist great power aspirations are likely to be more enduring than international interdependence and military rivalry, equally important as trade. So we have the paradox, where great

---

[13] An enforcement measure under the laws of armed conflict consisting of an act that would otherwise be lawful but which is justified as a response to the unlawful acts of the enemy.

powers are encircling each other with trade agreements, in a competitive frenzy for FTA's, but simultaneously they are encircling each other by political influence and military spending. The world seems delicately poised and it is not clear which of the two versions of international relations will win out. So the question is whether world leadership will be provided by leaders whose moral valuation of peace and the control of war's conduct will override all other values. Statecraft has never been a morality tale.

Can Nuclear weapon states expect a dramatic shift in the conduct of statecraft since nuclear weapons pose significant existential risks? One can only be optimistic from the current trend where significant spectrum of the global leadership is calling for reduction in nuclear weapons with global Zero as the vision. Nuclear stability is however an imperative need as long as nuclear weapons exist and must be maintained as the long road to zero is traversed.

Nuclear Stability

Nuclear instability is still a major cause of concern. A plethora of political and strategic factors add up to building nuclear instability. They include intensity of hostility between adversaries, particularly when one or more nuclear adversary states seek to alter the 'status quo'; the presence or absence of Allies (nuclear or major military allies) also contributes to nuclear instability. Internal political instability, owing to military takeovers and/or separatist movements; misperceptions by A or B of the other's intentions in a crisis and intelligence failure (e.g., on whether nukes have arrived to arm missiles and whether the local operators have been delegated the decision to fire nuclear-tipped missiles in self-defence, such as in the Cuban missile crisis); Size and technical differences can give rise to low credibility of deterrence posture—leading to deterrence instability. Intense hostility and domestic instability can accentuate crisis instability where the states do not trust each other and misread the other. The other angles on nuclear instability include crisis instability, arms race instability, continued proliferation and multiplication of nuclear powers and complex alignments.

The edifice of strategic stability based on nuclear deterrence is founded on the notion of mutual vulnerability. If nuclear vulnerability is perceived as non-existent by a particular state it may not be deterred except of course by other considerations that are seen to be disadvantageous. States therefore seek to maintain arsenals that preserve vulnerability. This proclivity then results in an action - reaction scenario resulting in arms race instability. This is exactly what happened during the cold war. The advent of missile defences has certainly muddied the waters of mutual vulnerability. The rationale for missile defences are today driven by the idea that the potential for nuclear weapons falling into hands of non deterrable entities like non state actors and states termed by the west as rogue states. Protection through missile defences is therefore considered a strategic necessity. So, as the deployment of missile defences gains pace, there will be a counter reaction to maintain the mutual vulnerability equation through the spread of missile defences and a concurrent increase in the nuclear arsenals of the contending states.

The major concern expressed by the United States, its allies and several other states, including India, was the proliferation of nuclear capability to non-state actors. The United States NPR 2010 expresses these concerns, "Before long we will be living in a world with a steadily growing number of nuclear armed states and an increasing likelihood of terrorists getting their hands on nuclear weapons. Therefore, for the first time, the 2010 NPR places this priority atop the nuclear agenda". The question is - will the emergence of these new threats that are outside the nuclear deterrence edifice, force a rethink about the manner in which the nuclear domain has been treated? Will it facilitate the removal of shibboleths that stand in the way of reduction of the salience of nuclear weapons as a necessary condition for progress in the arena of non proliferation and disarmament? Logically it should. But as we know, the old fears remain and practice of statecraft may not fully acknowledge the need to factor in the impact of nuclear weapons in relations between Nuclear Weapon States, especially during crisis situations. It may come about if enlightened world leaders can reconcile their national interests with the larger interests of mankind.

Nuclear terrorism has been identified as the new menace that could rear its ugly head on the nuclear stage. Since such non-state entities have no address and do not operate as legal actors within the international state system, they are practically undeterrable except through threats to the countries who host such entities. Non proliferation measures are therefore likely to be more effective. Currently, Pakistan presents the greatest danger in terms of nuclear terrorism but the NWS states have yet to act in a concerted manner to reduce the risks since geopolitical interests are incongruent.

Though none of the sources of strategic instability can be eradicated as long as nuclear weapons exist, it can at least be mitigated to some extent if No First Use is embraced by all nuclear powers. The United States with its overwhelming conventional capability has not done so. But the military bureaucracies in the United States see No First Use as increasing vulnerability to a first strike. The resistance to change is also derived from the fact that nuclear weapons are perceived as valuable for roles beyond the core deterrence role. This is so since nuclear threats are perceived to be useful in the realm of grand strategy as it can directly influence the mind of the opponent's political decision makers. This is a questionable assumption in a deterrent situation between nuclear armed states. For political decision makers base their decisions more on what they have to lose rather than what harm can be caused to the opponent. The United States' use of threats during the cold war is illustrative.

Several United States Presidents, Truman, Eisenhower, Kennedy, Johnson and Nixon considered the use of nuclear weapons against non nuclear states during periods of crises and war. In general in nearly all cases, the military advice was overruled by the political leadership. The decision of the political leadership was primarily based on the impact of nuclear use on reputational, tactical/strategic and moral considerations. The documentary evidence suggests that tactical or strategic considerations were not as significant for them as reputational and image considerations were.[14] It is difficult to fathom, why the United States with such overwhelming conventional superiority cannot embrace No First Use in the prevailing international security climate. One could surmise that declaration of No First Use by United States and Russia could catalyse

---

[14] T.V. Paul, *Tradition of Non-use of Nuclear Weapons*, Stanford University Press, California – Pgs.38-64

other nuclear weapon states to follow suit. It would be a major step in enhancing strategic stability and facilitating further reductions in nuclear weapons. NFU should also bury the perceived utility of tactical nuclear weapons.

Tactical nuclear weapons are also called sub-strategic since it causes restricted destruction in comparison to strategic weapons. Their use has been visualised to deter and if necessary blunt conventional attacks. Both the United States and Russia reportedly possess a fairly large numbers of tactical nuclear weapons. The utility of tactical nuclear weapons is based on questionable presumptions. It is presumed that the state which is at the receiving end will immediately realise that a tactical nuclear weapon has been used. The idea that weapons are tactical in itself is misplaced. Whether it is a tactical or strategic weapon will have to be determined by the impact it creates on the political and strategic situation. It is difficult to imagine that the use of tactical nuclear weapons will not have a strategic impact as the level of the exchange taking place will invariably be pushed towards a higher nuclear realm with speedy escalation beyond the fathomable cognitive powers of contending parties. There is no guarantee that the nuclear exchange that will follow will be restricted to the tactical realm. In fact the fog of war would take over and the conflict could quickly be pushed to a free for all exchange for uncertainty and fear would have engulfed decision makers and the "use them or lose them" idea would probably prevail. So, the idea that use of tactical weapon will assist in keeping nuclear exchange to low levels is based on military fiction that ignores military realities. The use of tactical weapons is most unlikely to pass the test of practical utility which is what determines its necessity.

NFU will also reduce the requirement of maintaining hair trigger postures which surely are the relics of the Cold War. Survivability of the nuclear arsenal is the key factor that shapes the form and content of nuclear structures. Deterrence is derived from the belief that survival of a low number of weapons is sufficient to deter due to the immense destruction it can cause. The artificial notion that targets can be divided neatly into counterforce and counter value is a delusion to detract from the inconvenient truth that nearly all targets will involve significantly large civilian causalities. It must also be admitted that command and control systems survivability is difficult but not impossible in acquiring the ability to absorb a first strike unless perhaps it is a "bolt from the blue attack" which implies, that the nuclear attack was launched without a concurrent deterioration in political relations. A scenario that is impossible to visualise until a large number of nuclear weapons has fallen into the hands of madmen out to destroy the world or it was an accidental launch.

Conclusion

Changed geopolitical realities provide the essential space for reducing the salience of nuclear weapons in the conduct of international relations. While there will never be a guarantee regarding the state of affairs in the future, not to seize the moment is akin to being victimized by the past. On the other hand, the lessons of the past, embedded in the Cold War history have actually found a voice that is now resonating globally. The call for action is from across the professional spectrum and includes politicians, military leaders, scientists et al. These are voices of the people who were the hands on practitioners of the dangerous game and their unanimous verdict is clear and unambiguous - abolish nuclear weapons and until then make them as safe and secure as possible, by reducing their role.

Core deterrence, No First Use and civilian control should be the cornerstones of nuclear doctrines to make the world safer and facilitate the long journey to global zero. This will reduce reliance on nuclear weapons. India and China are already in conformity with core deterrence, NFU and civilian control. The United States and Russia can surely show the way if the leadership can overcome the internal constituencies, especially the military bureaucracies that remain tethered to the Cold War paradigm, despite military realities and the attendant risks of nuclear war fighting. It should be feasible to get others to follow if United States and Russia lead by example and display political wills that accommodate national interests with the common good of mankind. The journey is certainly a herculean one, but it is a cause worth relentlessly pursuing.

No First Use as Strategic Doctrine

Swaran Singh[1]

No First Use (henceforth NFU) as a strategic doctrine is normally located in the midst of several similar political and military strategies that aim at making nuclear weapons less central to national security. Apart from ensuring strategic stability in perilous equations amongst nuclear adversaries, NFU also facilitates opening of new pathways for nuclear disarmament. In the military domain, these sets of strategies seek to ensure escalation-control and flexible response; and that nuclear weapons response is never triggered automatically, inadvertently, or based on misinformation or miscalculation. Political strategies in this genre seek to de-legitimise threat of use or actual use of nuclear weapons, de-incentivise their lure for non-nuclear weapons states; even stigmatise their possession by strengthening the norm of nuclear taboo.

In operative terms of administrating processes to achieve these goals, these strategies together aim to achieve nuclear disarmament through strengthening non-proliferation of nuclear materials and technologies and know-how; and thereby reduce and, if possible eliminate, any chances of access to these by the so-called aspiraning nuclear weapon powers, rogue state and non-state actors like terrorists. Theoretically, in the whole spectrum of 'non-use' of nuclear weapons, NFU falls in between the formulations of nuclear taboo on the one hand and 'negative security assurances' on the other. While non-use of nuclear weapons against non-nuclear weapons states remains the largely accepted norm in all nuclear weapons states, nuclear taboo has been effective only in practice. It means that while the norm of

[1] Author is Professor and Chairperson, Centre for International Politics, Organisation and Disarmament, School of International Studies, Jawaharlal Nehru University, New Delhi. E-mail: ssingh@mail.jnu.ac.in

nuclear taboo is reinforced with every day passing without actual use of nuclear weapons, not one state has adopted it as the guiding axiom of their war-fighting strategies.[2] Nuclear weapons, therefore, continue to be seen as weapons of last resort in war and as currency of power in peace times.

While some nuclear weapons states continue to justify their reluctance to eliminate their nuclear arsenals in the name of their extant threats, others talk of unforeseen exigencies that may emerge suddenly; and that they will not be able to immediately rebuild nuclear arsenals to deal with those exigencies. One answer to this dilemma lies in Thomas C. Schelling, who is known to see complex interdependence existing between apparently contradictory situations like obese not being foodie and he believes that for sustaining "non-use" of nuclear weapons, "evolution of that status [nuclear taboo] has been as important as development of nuclear arsenals."[3] And here, the strategic doctrine of NFU perhaps provides that critical link that can actualise Schelling's prophecy and square this circle of having nuclear weapons and ensuring their 'non-use' at the same time. Secondly, given that the rising mid-ranking nuclear weapons powers – like China and India – have persisted with their strong commitment to the NFU doctrine makes this pathway to nuclear disarmament increasingly visible and potent. Even Pakistan and North Korea have shown some inclination towards the NFU doctrine and this increasing acceptability provides hope to make NFU not only worth exploring but a feasible instrument to strengthen nuclear disarmament trends.

It is in this backdrop of sporadic attempts at universalising NFU as a strategic doctrine for all nuclear weapons powers that this chapter seeks to raise some of the larger questions. Do nuclear weapons have any military role in the post-cold war world other than being mere political weapons? Do they have any role at all in dealing with emerging contemporary existential threats like climate change, energy security, pandemics, piracy or terrorism? Especially, in face of the increasing burden of conventional defence systems and increasing internal security challenges, is it worthwhile

---

[2] Nina Tannenwald, *The Nuclear Taboo: The United States and the Non-Use of Nuclear Weapons*, (Cambridge: Cambridge University Press, 2007), p. 361.

[3] Nina Tannenwald, *Stigmatizing the Bomb: Origins of the Nuclear Taboo, International Security*, Vol. 29, no. 4 (Spring 2005), p. 6.

to maintain First Use doctrine with expensive command and control, high-alert and operational preparedness? And finally, if NFU makes such a convincing formulation for peace, why has it not been adopted by all nuclear weapons powers and why have multilateral campaigns for it been such non-starters? And since there are no unanimous answers to these questions available, this paper seeks to deconstruct some of these puzzles by examining the NFU related policies and postures of major nuclear weapons powers and from there crystal gaze NFU's future trajectories.

US and NATO opposition

To begin with, the United States (henceforth US) and North Atlantic Treaty Organisation (NATO) have been the two sworn opponents of the NFU maxim. US and therefore NATO, have always believed and continue to believe, in First Use of nuclear weapons though they swear by their 'non-use' against non-nuclear weapons states. In the early 1990s, when much of the world was debating about the 'peace dividends' at the end of Cold War, US and NATO were expanding the sway of their First Use paradigm, calling it a legitimate response to weapons of mass destruction, including chemical and biological weapons. This was being done in the name of these states no more in possession of chemical and biological weapons available with them while the so-called rogue states were suspected of keeping or developing these stockpiles. The US doctrine includes use of nuclear weapons to cover a range of exigencies like "core mission; as weapons of last resort; to discourage potential new nuclear weapons states; to deter use of non-nuclear weapons of mass destruction; and specialized, non-unique regional missions."[4] The George W. Bush Jr. presidency was to go a step further and the 2005 Joint Chiefs of Staff draft Joint Doctrine for Nuclear Operations suggested even 'pre-emptive' nuclear strikes.[5] It recommended the use of nuclear weapons to counter "imminent attack from adversary biological weapons" against "US, multinational, or alliance forces or civilian populations" which was seen as regressive.[6]

---

[4] Wolfgang K. H. Panofsky and George Buss, "The Doctrine of the Nuclear Weapon States and the Future of Non-proliferation", *Arms Control Today*, Vol. 24, No. 6 (July/Aug 1994), p. 7.

[5] Jonathan Power, "'No first use' debate heats up", *Khaleej Times*, 30 March 2011, p. 11.

[6] Nick Ritchie, *US Nuclear Weapons Policy after the Cold War: Russians, 'rogues' and domestic division*, (New York: Routledge, 2009), p. 65.

This, however, does not mean that the US and NATO have not had constituencies propagating the NFU maxim. Indeed, it is the American Baruch Plan of 1946 that is credited to having first propagated the 'non-use' and 'no-first-use' of nuclear weapons. This, of course, was to change with the Soviet detonation of the atom bomb in 1949. NATO allies wanted to be assured that US nuclear weapons were to get involved at a very early stage of conventional attack by the Soviet side. By 1954, the US had begun deploying tactical nukes on NATO's European frontlines as also had it changed its doctrinal formulation to say that nuclear weapons should be forbidden except in defence against aggression. It was only in the wake of US-Soviet détente and their first Strategic Arms Limitation Treaty (SALT) of 1972 that NFU maxim begun to emerge as superpower deliberations: that the purpose of nuclear weapons was only to prevent war, not to wage it. This was to strengthen their domestic debates in favour of NFU doctrine and by 1978, at the UN Special Session on Disarmament that year, US was ready to formally pledge not to use nuclear weapons against non-nuclear weapons states that are signatory to the NPT.[7] In November 1985, Reagan and Gorbachev said famously "a nuclear war cannot be won and must never be fought" which almost repudiated US First Use doctrine and was severely criticised at home.[8] Since then, though non-use maxim has been repeated on rare occasions, successive administrations have "maintained a policy of 'strategic ambiguity' refusing to rule out a nuclear response even to a biological and chemical attack."[9]

Within NATO's strategic doctrinal debates as well, while UK and France have been firm supporters of First Use of nuclear weapons, there have been powerful dissenting voices. To begin with, it was the nuclear freeze movements of early 1980s that had unleashed first serious debate on NATO shifting to NFU as its strategic doctrine.[10] Important members

---

[7] Lawrence D. Weiler, "No first use: a history" *Bulletin of the Atomic Scientists*, Vol. 39, no.2, (February 1983), p. 32.

[8] Allan S. Krass, "The People, The Debt, and Michail", *Bulletin of the Atomic Scientists*, Vol. 47, no. 9 (November 1991), p. 15.

[9] Eugene R. Wittkopf, Christopher Martin Jones, and Charles W Kegley, *American Foreign Policy: Pattern and Process*, (Belmonot, CA: Thomson Wadsworth, 2008), p. 94.

[10] John J. Mearsheimer, "Nuclear Weapons and Deterrence in Europe", *International Security*, Vol. 9, no. 3 (Winter 1984/85), p. 19.

like Germany, Canada and Belgium have since occasionally raised their voice on the need for debates on adopting NFU as NATO's strategic doctrine.[11] However, even after the collapse of former Soviet Union, when UK and France have no visible nuclear threats from any quarter, they still continue to cling to their First Use doctrine in the name of unforeseen exigencies.[12] The generally held belief though is that UK and France wish to retain their nuclear weapons and the First Use doctrine more for reasons of prestige and autonomy in international politics. Nevertheless, it is the US in the end that still determines NATO's tenor on these historic preferences. And the most recent major announcement by the US was their *Nuclear Posture Review* of April 2010 that says that "The United States will not use or threaten to use nuclear weapons against non-nuclear weapons states that are party to the NPT and *in compliance with their nuclear non-proliferation obligations* (emphasis added)."[13] This seems to have further shrunk the space for alternatives to First Use orthodoxy inside the US and NATO.

China's NFU Doctrine

In contrast to US and NATO, China has been projecting itself as the torchbearer of NFU doctrine right from the day it tested its first atomic device on 16th October, 1964. China has since been seeking NFU to be adopted by all other nuclear weapons powers. On repeated occasions, almost every ten years, including in its last White Paper on National Defence 2010, China has declared NFU to be its strategic doctrine, projecting it as defensive and retaliatory in nature: "The Chinese government hereby solemnly declares that China will never at anytime, or under any circumstances, be the first to use nuclear weapons."[14] This has been China's standard refrain in various forums at home and abroad and were also part

---

[11] "Germany Raises No-First-Use issue at NATO meeting", *Arms Control Today*, (November/December, 1998; Praful Bidwai and Achin Vanaik, *New Nukes: India, Pakistan and Global Nuclear Disarmament*, (New York: Interlink Books, 2000), p. 256.

[12] Camille Grand et al, *US-European Non-proliferation Perspectives*, (Washington DC: Center for Strategic & International Studies, April 2009), p. 7.

[13] Department of Defence, United States of America, *Nuclear Posture Review Report*, April 2010, p. ix.

[14] Alexander T. Lennon, *Contemporary Nuclear Debates: Missile defense, arms control, and arms races*, (Cambridge, MA: MIT Press, 2002), p. 160.

of China's first official speech at the United Nations in 1972 where it further exhorted: "If the United States and the Soviet Union really and truly want disarmament, they should commit themselves not to be the first to use nuclear weapons. This is not something difficult to do."[15]

However, China has refused to elucidate on some of the important counterfactuals. Especially China's occasional practices like conducing military exercise in nuclear environment as also statements by its mid-ranking officials have repeatedly raised suspicion, even alarm. At the top of this list remains speculations about China's possible showdown with US in Taiwan Straits which is expected to trigger China's giving up of its NFU doctrine.[16] Judging China's intentions from its capabilities has been another stream of analysis assessing its NFU credentials. And here, since the early 1980s – that coincided with the rise of China as a major power and collapse of former Soviet Union – China's NFU doctrine has been under greater scrutiny and these analyses allude to China's differing policy postures as also evolving doctrinal formulations. Thirdly, this is also the period since when nuclear deterrence is believed to be in operation in Sino-US equations. In this backdrop, China's NFU campaign has often been seen as an ineffective strategy (mere paper tiger) in view of China's capabilities.

It is commonplace today that till the early 1980s, China had no deployed inter-continental ballistic missiles and submarine launched ballistic missiles to overcome overwhelming first nuclear strike from its superpower adversaries.[17] From the early 1990s, in the wake of US prioritising building of ballistic missile defence systems (Reagan's Star Wars), small nuclear arsenal of China have again been viewed as very vulnerable to US first strike. In view of this, Chinese experts have been debating on various possible alternatives; from threatening proliferation to expansion on their nuclear arsenals, especially by using decoys, as also brainstorming new doctrinal formulations like limited war and flexible response which have cast doubts

[15] Richard H. Ullman, "No First Use of Nuclear Weapons, *Foreign Affairs*, July 1972.

[16] Chu Shulong and Rong Yu, "China: Dynamic Minimum Deterrence", in Muthiah Alagappa (Ed), *The Long Shadow: Nuclear Weapons and Security in 21ˢᵗ century Asia*, (Singapore: National University Press, 2009), p. 176.

[17] Yao Yunzhu, "China's policy on nuclear weapons and disarmament", in Olav Njolstad (ed), *Nuclear Proliferation and International Order: Challenges to the Non-proliferation Treaty*, (New York: Routledge, 2011), p. 255.

on China's commitment to the NFU doctrine.[18] Of particular significance amongst these, has been the question of China's continued silence on questions about whether China's NFU applies in case of territories claimed by China as her own, like Taiwan or Arunachal Pradesh in India and whether China considers these as nuclear weapons states or non-nuclear weapons states with regard to its NFU.[19]

It is interesting to note that in spite of its vigorous political campaign in favour of NFU, most western experts have, right from the beginning, "dismissed 'no first use' (NFU) pledges as unverifiable, unenforceable propaganda" by China and how it was only Indian strategists and military leaders who, grounded in Gandhian pacifism, had credited China's commitment to NFU doctrine.[20] Indeed, Indian scholars till date continue to mark that distinction of trusting (though broadly) China's NFU pledge and there have been suggestions on how India and China could begin their work towards universalising NFU doctrine by signing a bilateral NFU undertaking.[21] Knowing that China has increasingly impressive leverages in international decision-making, this is believed to be the most potent first step in facilitating universalising of the NFU maxim. While Indian experts pride on India's sustained contributions to nuclear disarmament debates, Chinese experts believe that China's increasing involvement will have transformative impact on 21st century nuclear regimes.[22] The former

---

[18] Michael S. Chase and Evan Medeirose, "China's Evolving Nuclear Calculus: Modernisation and Doctrine", in James Mulvenon and David M. Kinkelstein (eds.), *China's Revolution in Doctrinal Affairs: Emerging Trends in the Operational Art of the Chinese People's Liberation Army*, (Alexandria, Va.: CAN Corp, 2005), p. 121.

[19] George H. Quester, *Nuclear First Strike: Consequences of a Broken Taboo*, (Baltimore, Maryland: The Johns Hopkins University Press, 2006), p. 48; Swaran Singh, "China's Nuclear Deterrent", in Kanti P. Bajpai and Amitabh Mattoo (eds), *The Peacock and the Dragon: India-China Relations in the 21st Century*, (New Delhi: Har Anand Publications, 2000), p. 65.

[20] Lyle J. Goldstein, *Preventive Attack and Weapons of Mass Destruction: A Comparative Historical Analysis*, (Stanford, Ca: Stanford University Press, 2006), p. 107-108.

[21] Annpurna Nautiyal, *Challenges to India's Foreign Policy in the New Era*, (New Delhi: Gyan Publishing House, 2008), p. 192. This is also expected to resolve the confusion on whether China's NFU applies to India as it is not clear if China considers India as a Nuclear Weapon State or a Non-Nuclear Weapon State as India is not signatory to nuclear Non-Proliferation Treaty of 1970.

[22] Zhao Tong, "China's Role in Reshaping the Global Nuclear Non-Proliferation Regime", *St Antony's International Review*, Vol 6, no. 2, (February 2011), p. 67.

Soviet Union was the other major state that believed in NFU and in September 1994, Moscow had signed a Sino-Russian NFU and de-targeting agreement though Russia has since deserted its NFU commitment thus further weakening chances of expanding the Asian consensus on NFU maxim.

Russia's Strategic U-Turn

In its historic transformation from Soviet Union to the Russian Federation, Moscow's view on NFU took a strategic U-turn away from NFU maxim. Russia moved exactly in the opposite direction compared to what was expected of the great powers' nuclear doctrines, following the end of the Cold War. The new Russian leadership was to increase its reliance on nuclear weapons. It is important to underline the point that unlike the US, that has never questioned its First Use doctrine, the Soviet Union is now known to have supported the "no first use" pledge from the very beginning.[23] According to official archives now available to scholars, the most explicit NFU pledge was made by the Soviet leader, Leonid Brezhnev in 1982, during the Second Special Session of UN General Assembly on Disarmament.[24] A decade later, in 1993, Russian Federation's military doctrine was to drop this pledge.[25] In the year 2000, Russia was to further expand the sweep of its First Use doctrine and state that Russia reserves "the right to use nuclear weapons in response to the use of nuclear and other mass destruction weapons against Russia and its allies, as well as in response to a large scale conventional aggression."[26]

No doubt, the Russian U-turn is understandable in view of disintegration of Soviet armed forces, deterioration of relations with the

---

[23] Olga Oliker, Keith Crane, Lowell H. Schwartz, and Catherine Yusupov, *Russian foreign policy: sources and implications*, (Santa Monica: RAND Corporation, 2009), p. 163. For counterview see Peter Vincent Pry, *War Scare: Russian and America on the Nuclear Brink*, (Westport, Connecticut: Greenwood Publishing Group, 1999), p. 106.

[24] Joseph Rotblat, *The Long Road to Peace* [Preeceedings of the forty-eighth Pugwash Conference on Science and World], (London: World Scientific Publishing, 2001), p. 127.

[25] Serge Schmemann, "Russia Drops Pledge of No First Use of Atom Arms" *New York Times*, 5 November, 1993.

[26] Alexei Arbatov, "The Transformation of Russia's Military Doctrine in the Aftermath of Kosovo and Chechnya", in Gabriel Gorodetsky (ed.), *Russia Between East and West: Russian Foreign Policy on the Threshold of the Twenty-First Century*, (London: Frank Cass, 2003), p. 29.

West, especially NATO's peace-enforcements in Europe's ethnic conflicts, rise of US as unipolar superpower and Russia's rising internal security challenges and so on.[27] Russia's strategic decline, especially the rot in its conventional and nuclear arsenals was to necessitate greater reliance on nuclear weapons towards ensuring its power stature in the comity of nations. But this trend has continued to move further away from the NFU maxim. According to Russia's 2010 Military Doctrine, it is the "expansion of any foreign military presence in the proximity of the national territory, both on land and at sea, [that] is one of the principal "military threats" and possesses a real possibility of escalating into an armed conflict."[28] This, however, is projected to be an improvement on the alarming media stories that had followed the October 2009 interview of Russian Secretary of the Security Council, Nikolai Patrushev. Discussing, what was then Russia's draft Military Doctrine, Patrushev was quoted highlighting "preventive nuclear strikes against the aggressor" and this mention of 'preventive strikes' was alarming, coming in the aftermath of Russia's 2008 intervention in Georgia.[29]

More recent times have sure witnessed Russia returning to reducing the role of nuclear weapons. Compared to its March 2000 Military Doctrine, sanctioned use of nuclear weapons "in situations critical for national security" their 2010 Military Doctrine allows their use only in case when "the very existence of [Russia] is under threat."[30] This should open new spaces for enhancing Russia's comfort levels with NFU maxim. Also, more than this recent shift in its own Military Doctrine, Russia's leasing of six nuclear submarines and its contributions to India's own nuclear submarine program has made an important contribution to ensuring India's gradual progress

---

[27] Surya NarainYadav, *Nuclear Weapons and National Security: Emerging Challenges for Asia*, (New Delhi: Global Vision Publishing, 2009), pp. 29-32; Marcel Haas, *Russian Security and Air Power: 1992-2002*, (New York: Frank Cass, 2004), p. 61.

[28] James Kraska, *Arctic Security in an Age of Climate Change*, (New York: Cambridge University Press, 2011), p. 98.

[29] Jacob W. Kipp, "Russian Nuclear First Use: a Case of Self-Defeating Exaggeration?", in *The Jamestown Foundation*, 12 January, 2010 at http://www.jamestown.org/single/?no_cache=1&tx_ttnews%5Btt_news%5D=35902

[30] Nikolai Sokov, "The New, 2010 Russian Military Doctrine: The Nuclear Angle", *James Martin Center for Non-proliferation Studies* (CNS), 5 February 2010, accessed on 18 July 2011, at http://cns.miis.edu/stories/100205_russian_nuclear_doctrine.htm

towards building its second strike capability and thereby facilitating India's continued commitment to NFU maxim.

Evolution of India's NFU doctrine

India boasts of being one of the staunchest votaries of disarmament and, even with its limited visibility and resources at hand, had been a regular participant in various multilateral debates, if not actual negotiations. Serious thinking on adopting an NFU doctrine in case of India had begun to evolve from the late 1980s though it was formally announced as India's preference only in India's draft nuclear doctrine in August 1999. As India began developing air deliverable nuclear weapons from late 1980s, a select group of officials and advisers had worked out 'minimum deterrence' and 'NFU' as two broad parameters of India's nuclear doctrine.

However, India's practical experience as a state with nuclear weapons has also witnessed an evolution from idealism of disarmament to pragmatic postures of arms control and non-proliferation. India's U-turn on NPT presents an apt example to explain this rapid evolution of India's postures in all matters nuclear. Similarly, India's adaptation of NFU doctrine (in absence of a proven second strike capability) has faced tremendous criticism and this has partly triggered its evolution which remains another major case in point. For instance, India had declared the policy of NFU was outlined by Prime Minister Vajpayee during his speeches following India's nuclear tests of May 1998. These sounded very Nehruvian in tenor and implied that whatever the circumstance, India will not be the first to use nuclear weapons and that India will never use nuclear weapons against non-nuclear weapons states.[31]

This NFU doctrine of India had witnessed its first major evolution during the presentations of India's draft nuclear doctrine in August 1999 which seemed to emphasise on ensuring "nuclear retaliation to a first strike will be massive and designed to inflict unacceptable damage." This was further circumscribed in January 2004, at the time of announcement from

---

[31] For details, see Swaran Singh, "India's Nuclear Doctrine: Ten Years Since the Kargil Conflict", in Bhumitra Chakma (ed.), *The Politics of Nuclear Weapons in South Asia*, (Farnham: Ashgate, 2011), pp. 57-74.

the Prime Minister's office about establishment of National Command Authority which followed the US take on it and added two caveats to India's NFU Doctrine: India would now see use of nuclear weapons as a legitimate response to any attack involving use of chemical or biological weapons as also in case of any WMD attack on Indian forces abroad. More recently, media had highlighted the NFU doctrine being further marginalised in the National Security Advisor's October 2010 address to National Defence College where he only talked of "no first use against non-nuclear weapon states" though this was quickly denied.[32] So, in spite of occasional pressures, India remains committed to the NFU and its significance has especially increased in view of new nuclear weapons powers.

Puzzles of Israel, Pakistan, North Korea

Israel has been suspected to have been a nuclear weapon state from 1967 but has not yet claimed status of a nuclear weapons power. Israel, as a result, keeps silent on issues of nuclear weapons as also on issue of NFU doctrine for any comments by them could imply confirming or denying that it has nuclear weapons. But there have been allusions and insinuations and dominant amongst these is what Israel calls its Samson Option i.e. treating nuclear weapons as weapons of last resort where massive retaliation will be the key. But indirectly, Israel also mentions that it "would not be the first country to formally introduce nuclear weapons in the region" which is often criticised as a "spoof" of an NFU.[33] But at the same time this does allude to a strong constituency inside Israel if not their official doctrinal orientation towards NFU doctrine.

Pakistan represents another interesting case of clear-mindedness on First Use in view of preponderance of India's conventional superiority. However, even Pakistan has had moments of reflection or aberrations. President Zardari, for instance, was reported having said on November 22, 2008 that his country was ready to commit to NFU.[34] But the reactions

[32] Speech by NSA Shri Shivshankar Menon at NDC on "The Role of Force in Strategic Affairs" October 21, 2010 at http://www.mea.gov.in/mystart.php?id=530116584

[33] Brahma Chellaney, "Nuclear-Deterrent Posture", in Brahma Chellaney (ed.), *Security India's Future in the New Millennium*, (Hyderabad: Orient Longman, 1999), p. 195.

[34] C. Christine Fair et al, *Pakistan: Can the United States Security an Insecure State?* (Santa Monica: RAND Corporation, 2010), p. 121.

from Pakistan showed that this was not any serious proposition and Pakistan has never formally subscribed to the NFU doctrine. It is generally General Khalid Kidwai, who is cited as the last word on Pakistan's nuclear doctrine. And now WikiLeaks have revealed how in the assessment of US Ambassador to Pakistan, Anne Patterson, "[A]lthough he has remained silent on the subject, [Army Chief, General] Kayani does not support Zardari's statement last year to the Indian press that Pakistan would adopt a 'no first use' policy on nuclear weapons."[35] But comments by President Zardari do establish the fact that even in Pakistan there exist pro-NFU doctrine constituencies that can be further cultivated.

North Korea remains the most difficult puzzle of all. Reportedly they have pronounced that their nuclear weapons are only meant to ensure their security against any nuclear blackmail and threat or use of nuclear weapons. While demonstrating their nuclear capability in October 2006, Pyongyang had announced that it "will never use nuclear weapons first."[36] But experts continue to debate about the nature of regime, the credibility of its nuclear weapons and whether its nuclear tests were successful at all. Needless to say, in reality North Korean nuclear weapons have had impressive political fallout and Pyongyang has been able to deter threats and incentivise engagement by great powers including US. Accordingly, North Korea will have to be part of any global NFU campaign or convention.

Universalising NFU

Thus far it appears that all nuclear weapon states have (or have had) their share of domestic constituencies, debating (if not propagating) a need for a NFU doctrine. In some states like China and India, and even North Korea, Israel, and Pakistan, there may be the need to encourage such stakeholders. So, it seems this is going to be a bottom-up initiative led by China and India but in close cooperation with other major stakeholders even in non-nuclear weapons states like Japan, Australia, Canada, Sweden and even

---

[35] Agencies, "Kayani does not support Zardari 'no-first-use' N-policy: Wikileaks", *Indian Express*, posted 6 May 2011 at http://www.indianexpress.com/news/kayani-does-not-support-zardaris-nofirstuse-npolicy-wikileaks/786878/

[36] John S. Park and Dong Sun Lee, "North Korea: Existential Deterrence and Diplomatic Leverage", Muthiah Allagappa (ed.), *The Long Shadow: Nuclear Weapons and Security in 21ˢᵗ Century Asia*, (Singapore: NUS Press, 2009), p. 279.

inside Russia and US. Secondly, these initiatives will have to rely on such earlier efforts. It is important to underline that first major step towards universalising NFU was taken in the 1950 World Council of Peace at Stockholm which concluded a *Stockholm Appeal,* proclaiming first use of atomic weapons to be committing a crime against humanity and the country that launched such a strike would be treated as a war criminal. The Appeal managed to obtain over 6.5 million signatures and triggered debates on how NFU doctrine moves towards elimination of nuclear weapons.[37]

In more recent times, the 2009 *Report of the International Commission on Nuclear Non-proliferation and Disarmament* repeatedly talks of need for universalising NFU as a critical step towards nuclear disarmament.[38] The report reposes faith in post-Cold War trends of vertical disarmament making minimal deterrence and NFU a far more credible strategic doctrine leading to changes in nuclear doctrines and force structures. It is expected that cold war mind sets of treating Soviet NFU as nothing but propaganda and scepticism about Chinese commitment and Indian proposition should give way to possible evolving consensus on NFU becoming a pathway to nuclear disarmament. On more specific terms, Alan Dowty talks of the UN Security Council taking the lead in expanding its Resolution 255 (of 19 June 1968) – that stipulated any nuclear attack on a non-nuclear state requiring it to come to the aid of the victim – and providing for similar protection against any first use of any of the WMD. This could be followed by agreements amongst nuclear weapons powers to the NFU leading to 'minimum deterrence' becoming the norm. To quote –

> The Universalisation of "no first use" could then serve as a platform for further progress toward the ultimate goal: the reduction and elimination of all WMD. Once these weapons serve no purpose but to deter the use of like weapons, their elimination, assuming adequate verification, would not threaten the legitimate security interests of any nation.[39]

---

[37] James J. Orr, *The Victim as Hero: Ideologies of Peace and National Identity in Post-war Japan,* (Manoa: University of Hawaii Press, 2001), p. 45.

[38] Gareth Evans and Yoriko Kawaguchi, *Eliminating Nuclear Threats: A Practical Agenda for Global Policymakers,* (Canberra: Paragon, 2009), pp. 177-178.

In the context of India, scholars like P.M. Kamath talk of the long term advantages of NFU doctrine or NFU Convention.[40] Apart from being militarily sustainable, NFU for him is a more democratic doctrine as it ensures civilian control on nuclear weapons instead of having to authorise commanders in the field for ready-to-shot operations. It seems strange that the most powerful proponent of democracy has also been the greatest proponent of the First Use doctrine while the so-called authoritarian regime has been the consistent supporter of NFU so far. Not just that, the US has gone out of its way to discourage its friends and allies from even debating on the No First Use and has even used pressure tactics to silence such propositions.

Joseph Rotblat has been arguing how, if each of the nuclear weapon powers commits not to use nuclear weapons of first strike, there shall be no occasion to use them at all, and how this can facilitate disarmament. Raja Mohan[41] believes that NFU doctrine remains premised on the belief that (a) more not better, if less is enough, (b) rejection of tactical nuclear weapons as weapons of instability, (c) need to forswear brinkmanship at the very early stages of conflict, (d) to avoid need for a hair-trigger reaction as basis of deterrence, (e) to keep warheads and deliver systems separate and thereby ensure their safety during first strike. It is based on this perspective that India has been able to sustain its commitment in campaigning for an international NFU Convention as a means for general and complete nuclear disarmament.

Conclusion

For a worst case assessment, for each nuclear weapon power, NFU doctrine pledge implies taking a grave political responsibility to choose to absorb the first nuclear strike. To facilitate nations making such a pledge, nuclear weapons powers could begin by taking few agreeable baby-steps like mutual

---

[39] Alan Dowty, "Making "No First Use" Work: Bring All WMD Inside the Tent", *Nonproliferation Review*, (Spring 2001), p. 84.

[40] P. M. Kamath, *Indian Policy of No First Use of Nuclear Weapons: Relevance to Peace and Security in South Asia*, (New Delhi: Anamika Publishers, 2009), p. 95.

[41] C. Raja Mohan, "No First Use and India's Nuclear Transition", *Pugwash Meeting No. 279* on 'No First Use of Nuclear Weapons' at http://www.pugwash.org/reports/nw/rajamohan.htm

de-alerting, de-targeting, de-activating their nuclear weapons and their delivery systems. Such initiatives could, in the long run, assist nuclear weapons powers as also non-nuclear nations arriving at regional and/or multilateral NFU understandings or even a global NFU Convention. Even before they achieve a NFU convention and establish it as a universal norm, such initiatives in that direction will be important for ensuring deterrence-stability amongst nuclear weapons powers that still believe in First Use nuclear doctrine.

Moreover, as it seems to be an extremely difficult proposition for each participating country, a NFU doctrine and especially a NFU Convention is going to throw up its own new challenges. As first thing, it will make the US conventional military superiority far more pronounced and smaller states like North Korea or Iran will be losing their capacity to deal with potential arm twisting. Conversely, any country that chooses to cheat will be able to hold hostage any great power, including the US. So even if US were to lead the NFU debate, the second tier nuclear weapons powers as also new nuclear aspirants may have no incentive to give up their nuclear weapons and may indeed be sceptical of the US' motives. Even the responses from Russia and China are likely to be cautious and defensive. For Russia and China, nuclear weapons remain important instruments of their power position. Similarly, initiatives from countries like China and India would make Russia and US feel that they are trying to achieve parity. Especially countries like the UK and France, that have never supported NFU and continue to support it even after the collapse of former Soviet Union, may fear losing their stature, compared to these emerging Asian countries.

To sum up, the difficulty seems primarily of a trust-deficit. Only sustained political campaign and specific baby-steps, including unilateral gestures by nuclear weapon powers, can create the atmospherics for substantive initiatives. Nuclear weapons powers adopting NFU as their strategic doctrine could be the first major stage for universalising NFU norm and this has to be accompanied by genuine disarmament by all parties. Before asking nations to sign any new agreements, focussing on implementing the three major objectives of so-called universalised and time-tested nuclear Non-Proliferation Treaty (NPT) – i. e. disarmament by nuclear weapons states, non-proliferation to new states, and opening greater access to civilian nuclear technologies amongst non-nuclear countries – would allow strategic visions to begin focussing on the positive side of nuclear science. Evolving such a larger vision on nuclear science may facilitate putting in place this narrow obsession with nuclear deterrence theologies and herald a real Nuclear Age that stands distorted for being born in the midst of the most destructive war of human history.

Through the Techno-Political Maze

G. Balachandran

The period 2007-2009 is a milestone in the journey towards eliminating nuclear weapons. A cascade of global nuclear disarmament proposals has emerged from different sources. Researchers at the James Martin Centre for Non-proliferation Studies identified some 42 proposals in the period from 1995 to 2009. The emphatic call for leadership in nuclear disarmament from US and Russia made in 2007 and in 2008 by the Schultz-Kissinger-Perry-Nunn quartet, was taken up by similar calls by Mr. Gorbachev and a number of former Defence Ministers and Generals which captured global attention. This has been followed by influential non governmental groups being formed to build global opinion and provide momentum to nuclear disarmament. The arrival of President Obama on the global scene, with a commitment to a world without nuclear weapons, has further energised the discourse. The promise of re-starting the US-Russia negotiations to further reduce their nuclear arsenals is being viewed as a major sign of a new phase in nuclear disarmament.

The Weapons of Mass Destruction Commission led by Hans Blix had produced a fine report with a set of pragmatic recommendations. It is now followed by the International Commission on Nuclear Non Proliferation & Disarmament brought into being by the Australian and Japanese governments. In 2008, the European Union had outlined an Eight Point initiative to the UN Secretary General. The same year, UN Secretary General, Ban Ki Moon delivered a major and meaningful address on Nuclear Disarmament. It was the first ever such address by a UN Secretary General, exclusively on nuclear disarmament. These initiatives take the nuclear disarmament discourse well beyond the earlier attempts of the 1990s. The '13 Practical Steps' on the implementing Article VI of the NPT, resolutions offered by Japan, Myanmar, the New Agenda Coalition form part disarmament proposals before the turn of the Century. The 2010 Global Zero plan significantly contributes towards a phased and verifiable elimination of all nuclear weapons is a four-phased strategy to reach a global zero accord over 14 years (2010–2023) and to complete the dismantlement of all remaining nuclear warheads, over the following seven years (2024–2030).

There are some prerequisites to achieve this; (i) political consensus on the part of NWS for a nuclear weapon free world (ii) consensus amongst the national security agencies of both NWS and NNWS that a nuclear-weapon-free world does not have negative consequences for their national security i.e. no security threat from conventional forces, (iii) consensus amongst national science and technical agencies in the NWS that nuclear disarmament is verifiable and maintainable, (iv) absence of "rogue" states attempting to clandestinely develop nuclear explosive devices and (v) an established and well defined obligation for dealing with violation of legal obligations and commitments.

The current scenario is such that many of the major substantive requirements of these proposals have been implemented in spirit if not in letter and there is a reduction in the nuclear arsenals of the erstwhile superpowers. In the CTBT there exists a moratorium on nuclear testing by all the nuclear weapon states since 1998 with the exception of one maverick/rogue state. As for the FMCT, a moratorium on production of fissile material for nuclear explosive purposes by four of the nuclear weapon states and slow accretion of nuclear explosive material by others, with one exception, is prevalent.

There is some progress in some of the other non-quantifiable elements such as "transparency in arsenals", "diminishing the strategic role of nuclear weapons" etc.

With almost all proposals focussing on disarmament, there is very little, if any, progress on other elements of the prerequisites for global nuclear disarmament such as stronger international non-proliferation norms, stronger international rules for verification of treaty compliances, effective checks on safeguards violations, with appropriate mechanisms for international action to penalise the violator and restore status quo ante, or even effective legal mechanisms to reduce or nullify the negative consequences that the withdrawal of parties from international treaties will have, pertaining to international peace .

The Future of Disarmament

Complete nuclear disarmament is not feasible unless NWS are assured that in respect of all NNWS, there is neither diversion of declared nuclear material from peaceful nuclear activities nor any indication of any undeclared nuclear material or activities; in short all nuclear material remained in peaceful activities. Such a conclusion cannot be drawn in the absence of much stronger and legally enforceable non-proliferation and inspection regime. This regime will be difficult to achieve in the absence of a belief on the part of NNWS that the NWS states are committed to complete nuclear disarmament, based on objective norms, not necessarily time bound, but linked to specific goals.

Based on this, it is safe to conclude that disarmament and non-proliferation go hand-in-hand. The level of nuclear disarmament should be linked to the level of assurance of absence of non-peaceful material or activities in NNWS i.e. when there is complete assurance that there is no non-peaceful nuclear material or activities in any NNWS. In addition, there must be in place, strong international norms on non-proliferation norms and legally enforceable actions against states violating such norms to undo the damage and prevent in future, such violations.

The Techno-Political Maze

In order to arrive at disarmament in technical advances for verification, technologies are essential. As a recent NAS report pointed out, while technologies for monitoring and verification of declared nuclear material and weapons are available, such technologies for undeclared nuclear material are yet to be developed. That is a technical issue. However, even when such technologies become available, their application would require NNWS to accept stronger and more intrusive inspection regimes. Acceptance of such conditions by NNWS is a political issue. In the meantime, in the absence of total nuclear disarmament, the propensity to develop, in a clandestine manner, nuclear explosive devices will still exist. The reasons for such activities are political. On the other hand, such activities have to be conducted in such a manner that they are not discovered. That is a technological issue.

Future prospects

Any progress in the near future towards total nuclear disarmament will be dependent on the progress of international advances in the non-proliferation regime, in particular on technological advances to detect undeclared nuclear materials and facilities. These, in turn, will require far greater intrusive international verification protocols; NNWS's acceptance of such technologies and intrusive inspections will depend, by and large, on the faith these States have on the sincerity of the NWS's commitment to complete nuclear disarmament. All of this in turn depends on the NNWS's acceptance of such technologies and intrusive inspections- a classic case of chicken and the egg or the "hole in the bucket" calypso song. Therefore, a strict time-bound disarmament plan is unlikely to be fully successful-as has been evident from the failure of such past proposals.

In the short term, some action by NWS would serve to inspire confidence in their commitment, in the following ways:

(i) To accept safeguards regime in line with those accepted by the NNWS i.e. to ensure non-diversion of civil nuclear material and facilities for nuclear explosive purposes. At the moment, the NPT NWS have safeguards agreements that allow them to withdraw nuclear materials and facilities, listed for safeguards, as and when they choose. However with a moratorium on fissile material production for nuclear explosive purposes, with a formal FMCT under discussion they can now subject themselves to the same safeguards system in respect of their civil nuclear facilities as those in respect of NNWS.

(ii) In time, they can also accept the same degree of conformity in respect of the Additional Protocol.

(iii) Seriously negotiate amongst them and engage the NNWS as well, on some of the other common themes present in the major past disarmament proposals such as NSA (Negative Security Assurances, De-alerting, Doctrinal changes i.e reducing further the relevance of nuclear weapons etc.

(iv) More generally to aim for international nuclear norms that are universal and non-discriminatory.

On the other hand, NNWS actions to inspire confidence about their commitment to non-proliferation could entail the incorporation of the non-proliferation requirements in their proposals for nuclear disarmament as well as engage in a more responsible manner with the NWS and nuclear technology suppliers, on the need for control of nuclear technology transfers.

Technological dimensions: Proliferation activities

There exist certain routes for nuclear explosive devices- (a) HEU- Highly Enriched Uranium and (b) Pu- Plutonium; Pu is not a naturally occurring element and one needs natural Uranium for production of Pu. HEU too is not a naturally occurring element, requiring natural uranium for enrichment. Hence, access to natural uranium is an essential pre-requisite for any effort to develop nuclear explosive devices. Furthermore, both HEU and PU production need access to or knowledge of sensitive technologies. These are scientific and technological development in NNWS, coupled with rapid dissemination of dual-use technologies along with globalisation of manufacturing activities.

Natural Uranium

- Uranium ore widely disbursed. Nearly 40 states have so far mined uranium ore indigenously;

- More than 75 countries have invested resources in uranium exploration and development activities;

- Countries with Identifiable uranium resources: nearly 50;

- New and novel techniques for production of uranium-such as extraction of uranium from sea water;

- Uranium ores and ore processing to produce Yellow cake not under current safeguards regime;

- Minimal or modest quantities of natural uranium needed for manufacturing a nuclear explosive device- (a) HEU: 4.4-7.2 MT and (b) Pu- approximately 8 MT.

- International assistance available for exploration of uranium resources and mining – IAEA TC (Technical Cooperation) projects, for example.

Proliferation activities through the Nuclear Explosive device route:

- HEU- natural Uranium ore- conversion- enrichment- device

- Pu-natural uranium- conversion- fuel fabrication-reactors to produce spent fuel- reprocessing plants to separate PU- non-nuclear related technologies- device.

Proliferation activities- Conversion facilities:

- Small and even pilot plant scale facilities sufficient for conversion of natural uranium to uranium compounds essential for either enrichment or fuel fabrication.

- Conversion facilities are covered under current IAEA safeguards regime-applicable to almost all of the current NNWS.

Proliferation activities

Different enrichment technologies have different technical and proliferation related characteristics:

(1) Calutron-EMIS (Electro Magnetic Isotope Separation)

(2) Gaseous Diffusion

(3) Chemical Exchange

(4) Centrifuge

(5) Laser- AVLIS

Nonproliferation Characteristics of Various Enrichment Processes

	Proliferation Sensitivity	Detectability (Selected (Criteria)		
		Size	Energy Consumption	Wide Area EM
Calutron / EMIS	(hight)	Yes	Yes	Yes
Gaseous Diffusion	low	Yes	Yes	Yes
Chemical Exchange	Very low	(Yes)	(No)	(Yes)
Centrifuge	(high)	No	NO	No
Laser	(high)	No	NO	NO

Alexander Glaser: Life in a Nuclear Powered Crowd
New Approaches to Cooperative Security Workshop Jaye River Conference Center, Queenstown, Maryland, June 13-15, 2005

From a proliferation perspective, Centrifuge technology and laser isotope separation technologies offer the best means to evade detection of clandestine and undeclared enrichment facilities. It is well established and currently the most widely used technology. Historically this has been the route so far- Pakistan, Iran, A.Q. Khan network- involving a multi-country manufacturing and fabrication facilities; Amenable to productivity improvements through nominal investments in technology development- Pakistan and Iran for example. Laser isotope separation is far more complex and requires major and substantial technological challenges to overcome.

Figure 1

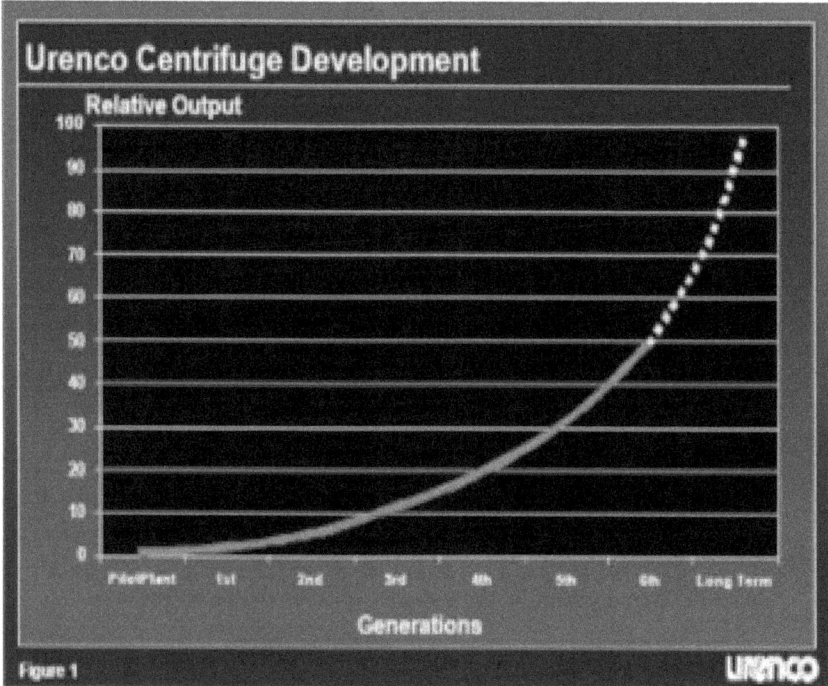

Enrichment: The Urenco example

Alexander Glaser: Life in a Nuclear Powered Crowd
New Approaches to Cooperative Security Workshop, Wye River Conference
Centre, Queenstown, Maryland, June 13-15, 2005

Centrifuge Generations

Level of Technology	Rotor Material	kg SWU/yr (estimated)	Deployment	Examples
Low	Aluminum	2	1970's	Pakistan P-1 (Netherlands D-1)
Medium	Maraging Steel	5	1980's	Pakistan P-2 (Germany G-2)
Medium	Carbon Fiber (Subcritical Machine)	10	?	Russia
High	Carbon Fiber	40	1990's	Urenco TC-12
High	Carbon Fiber	100	2000's	Urenco TC-21
High	Carbon Fiber	200-300	2000's	Usec Set III/V

Note: Reportedly the following machines are Similar (as they are based no the Dutch D-1): Pakistan P-1, Iran I-1 and Libya L-1

Enrichment: The Urenco example

(1) Urenco Capacity 2009   =   12200 tSW

(2) Urenco deliveries 2009   =   11800 tSW

(3) Production 2009 (TC12 equivalent)   =   52049

(4) TC12 capacity (approximate)   =   230 SWU

(5) Energy consumption Urenco 2009   =   37 Mwh/tSW

                                            =   37 Kwh/SWU

Laser enrichment:

(1) Energy consumption per SWU much less than in case of centrifuge technology approximately by a factor of 3.

(2) SWU density higher than in case of centrifuge technology.

Technological dimensions: The Nuclear explosive device-Pu route

There are even more steps to manufacture nuclear explosive devices viz:

- Mining of uranium ore;

- Ore processing;

- Conversion;

- Enrichment if used as fuel for LWRs;

- Heavy water plants, if used as natural uranium fuel for PHWRs;

- Reprocessing plants;

- Development of additional technologies for the non-nuclear systems and components needed for explosive device fabrication;

- More expensive because of need to build additional facilities such as heavy water plants, or reprocessing facilities.

Less favourable opportunities however arise in concealing facilities from non-onsite monitoring and verification technologies.

Political Dimensions:

The compulsions, politically, are immense in terms of the Timeline challenges, that can be bolstered by strengthening the international verification regime by making signing and ratification of Additional Protocol compulsory. Current IAEA safeguards under INFCIRC/153 only will not enable IAEA to certify the absence of non-peaceful nuclear activities in NNWS. On the other hand, with AP in place, IAEA has been able to certify the absence of such activities in 52 of the 96 NNWS that have an AP in place- amongst them 31 of the 41 NNWS, with significant nuclear activities (SNA), including such NNWS as Canada, Japan, and Republic of Korea. An ever greater attempt should be made in persuasion with NNWS who currently do not have an AP in place, especially those that have SNA such as Algeria, Argentina, Brazil, Iran, Egypt, Syria, to sign and ratify the AP. To provide additional funding to IAEA, it would be significant for increased safeguards implementation in all the civil facilities in NWS, as well as engage in scientific and technical development of advanced verification and monitoring technologies. By strengthening the IAEA's powers to take actions against non-compliant states, without elaborate, time consuming and ineffective international sanctions procedures, much can be attained. Make IAEA's operations and reports more transparent- for example it is not in the public domain as to what criteria IAEA uses to certify either non-diversion of safeguarded material for non-peaceful purposes or absence of non-peaceful nuclear activities in NNWS; expand IAEA's TC (Technical Cooperation) programs with additional funding; make IAEA TC programs with proliferation implications, such as assistance for uranium exploration and uranium mining conditional upon AP- Pakistan, for example, benefited from a number of IAEA TC programs' assistance on such activities.

Furthermore, the NNWS can be persuaded on the need to restrict sensitive technologies in the absence of strong economic or commercial justification for such technologies. Also, establish under a transparent and non-discriminatory framework, mechanisms for an international fuel bank for nuclear power generation in NNWS. These initiatives can take the nuclear disarmament process beyond the earlier attempts of the 1990s.

Geopolitical Conditions Enabling Nuclear Disarmament

Ian Anthony

Introduction

The past three years have seen a sustained effort by Russia and the United States to restore arms control as one useful instrument that can help to create a more stable and peaceful international system. This effort bore fruit in April 2010, when Russia and the US signed a new Strategic Arms Reduction Treaty (the new START). At the end of March 2011, when the Bilateral Consultative Commission (BCC) on the new START met for the first time in Geneva, it was a reminder that the United States and Russia—the two countries that own the lion's share of nuclear weapons—had restored the process of step-by-step nuclear arms reductions inside a legal regime, with full verification.

At the end of 2010, there appears to be a period of consolidation as the agreement gets implemented and the main parties consider their next steps. This slowing of momentum does not mean inaction. Russia and the United States published aggregate data about the number of strategic offensive arms in their arsenals, drawn from the biannual exchange of data required by the Treaty. In that way, they recognised their obligation to be transparent in their actions, to reassure the wider international community that promises were being kept.

Building on the concept of reassurance through transparency, at the end of June 2011, the five permanent members of the UN Security Council (who are also the countries considered nuclear weapon states in the context of the Treaty on Non-proliferation of Nuclear Weapons (NPT)) met for a second time to consider issues of nuclear weapon-related transparency, verification and confidence-building. The P5 appear to have established an open-ended process of discussion of strategic stability in their relations.

For many years, the Russian government requested a new legally binding framework to govern the bilateral strategic nuclear relationship with the United States. The Bush Administration, while unenthusiastic about this idea, did eventually agree to codify reductions in deployed weapons in the Treaty on Strategic Offensive Reductions (SORT or the Moscow Treaty) after 2003, but without intrusive provisions for verification and, perhaps even more importantly for Russia, without any mechanism for sustained high-level strategic dialogue. Far from accomplishing Russian objectives, if anything, this arrangement confirmed to Moscow that strategic relations with Russia were now a second or even third order priority for the United States. The momentum in nuclear arms control can be attributed, at least in part, to a major political effort by the United States to demonstrate that it would be a serious partner in nuclear arms control, galvanized by the personal attention of President Barack Obama—whose contribution actually pre-dates his entering office.

At an open air meeting in July 2008 in Berlin, candidate Obama, as he then was, laid out his thinking on international affairs. At the point in his speech where he said that 'this is the moment when we must renew the goal of a world without nuclear weapons' Obama received a sustained and spontaneous ovation from the crowd, which numbered in the hundreds of thousands.[1] When President Obama returned to Europe and delivered a new set piece speech, in Prague in April 2009, he called the existence of thousands of nuclear weapons 'the most dangerous legacy of the Cold War' and proposed a three-pronged strategy for dealing with it.

As a first step towards 'a world without nuclear weapons' the President pledged that the US would reduce the role of nuclear weapons in its own national security strategy and urge others to do the same while also seeking an agreement with Russia on arms reductions. However, while noting the importance of deep arms reductions by the US and Russia, Obama

---

[1] The full text of the speech in Berlin by Barack Obama on July 24, 2008 can be found at URL http://edition.cnn.com/2008/POLITICS/07/24/obama.words/

underlined that this objective could not be reached quickly—including his memorable qualification 'perhaps not in my lifetime'.[2]

There is every indication that key players (first and foremost Russia) are unenthusiastic about follow-up negotiations on further nuclear arms reductions in the near term. Implementation of the new START without further reductions can be seen as a step towards the abolition of nuclear weapons, but it could equally be presented as preserving nuclear weapons as a central feature of the international security environment—albeit with fewer numbers and in an altered configuration.

In Prague, President Obama suggested that two other objectives were within reach in a much shorter time frame than disarmament, namely securing global stockpiles of the fissile material (without which it is impossible to make a nuclear explosive device) and finding an effective strategy to address the most serious nuclear proliferation challenges (including dismantling global trafficking networks). These were objectives to be met within the lifetime of an Obama Presidency.

It is possible to point to some improvement compared to the situation in 2008, in the area of non-proliferation. When the UN Secretary General outlined a five-point proposal for achieving a world free of nuclear weapons in October 2008, his initiative came at a particularly low point in the international politics of nuclear arms control.[3] For a number of years it had become routine for different groups of states to use the various weaknesses of the present system to criticize and attack each other, while trying to draw attention away from their own faults. At events like the 2005 NPT Review Conference and the UN World Summit meeting, the complaints of countries like Egypt and Iran against the established nuclear powers were immediately met by complaints from the US and others about the failure of the NPT to provide foolproof ways of catching and stopping proliferation. The results were entirely negative for all parties and practically nothing was achieved, even in the less controversial and more practical

---

[2] The speech delivered by President Barack Obama on April 9, 2009 can be found at URL http://prague.usembassy.gov/obama.html

[3] Ban Ki Moon, *The United Nations and Security in a Nuclear-Weapon-Free World*, Address to the East-West Institute, October 24, 2008, UN document SG/SM/11881 DC/3135, available at URL http://www.un.org/News/Press/docs/2008/sgsm11881.doc.htm

fields of cooperation.

Against this benchmark, the 2010 Review Conference of the NPT was seen as a relative success because it managed to produce a final document that included action plans on nonproliferation, disarmament, and peaceful uses of nuclear energy and a procedure for implementing a decision, calling for a WMD free zone in the Middle East that had been on the table since 1995, without action.

As with disarmament, there is a similar lack of clarity over how to interpret the current situation in relation to non-proliferation. Programs to build an advanced nuclear fuel cycle under national control are hard to distinguish from the steps that would be needed to create a key element in a nuclear weapon capability. Actions by North Korea showed that sensitive activities such as uranium enrichment and fuel reprocessing, undertaken for ostensibly civilian purposes may actually be applied in military programs and there is no shared understanding of how to interpret such sensitive projects in relation to non-proliferation commitments. The widespread concern over activities being carried out in Iran are a reminder that even if sensitive activities take place under external monitoring through IAEA safeguards, there may be no full assurance of peaceful intent.

The 2010 NPT Review Conference outcome does not provide a yardstick because although states did not behave as badly as they had in 2005, the agreed 'action plans' do not contain any measurable commitments. The plans were a recommitment to the basic elements of the NPT, combined with an exhortation to 'do better'. Convening a conference, probably in 2012, to discuss the WMD free zone in the Middle East, would meet the only measurable action required by the 2010 Conference. However, if that conference does not lead to any meaningful conclusions, it will undoubtedly be seen as a serious setback by at least some key NPT participating states.

Taking a twenty year perspective, the role of nuclear weapons in international security has undoubtedly been reduced in the period after the end of the Cold War. Countries that previously relied on nuclear weapons as the main plank in national strategy have pushed them to the back of their strategic thinking as to the method of ensuring security. The number of countries about which there are serious proliferation concerns, has also diminished.

In 1991, there was concern about the possible emergence of a relatively large number of new nuclear armed states, including Argentina, Brazil, Belarus, the Democratic People's Republic of Korea (DPRK or North Korea), Iran, Iraq, Kazakhstan, Libya, Ukraine, South Africa and Syria. By 2011, the risks had been lowered dramatically in one way or another in almost all of these countries. It is true that three countries have tested nuclear weapons since the end of the Cold War. However, two of these (India and Pakistan) were demonstrating a long-assumed capability that was already factored into the security calculations of most states. North Korea can be said to be the only country that truly crossed the nuclear weapon threshold after the end of the Cold War and even here, there are residual doubts about whether the DPRK has turned its demonstrated capability to conduct a nuclear explosion into a deliverable weapon.

This is perhaps a good time to look back over a decade, roughly, to try to find some additional context and perspective that will provide a better understanding of recent events.

An overview of developments in disarmament and non-proliferation

In the first decade, after the end of the Cold War, projects to roll back nuclear ambitions were largely accomplished, peacefully and through cooperation. However, this record of achievement has become more difficult to interpret during the second post-Cold War decade. Recent counter-proliferation efforts have been the result of more direct and coercive means that could put a question mark on the sustainability of progressive de-nuclearisation. These efforts have been accompanied by continuous investment in new and more advanced conventional military capabilities in the United States, in particular. Other countries that might see a future risk that they could be targets of counter-proliferation may already be putting in place, mitigation strategies, which could lead to not just a loss of momentum but backsliding on past achievements.

Disarmament

Roughly a decade ago, in 2000, the Review Conference of the NPT had agreed on thirteen practical steps that would represent a systematic and progressive nuclear disarmament.[4] The "13 steps", which were built on a set of Principles and Objectives for Nuclear Non-Proliferation and Disarmament agreed in the framework of the NPT in 1995, provided an agreed disarmament "roadmap" at the end of a decade in which, many, very real achievements in the field of arms control, could be listed.[5]

The 1991 Strategic Arms Reduction Treaty (START) had entered into force in 1994 and Russia and the United States were working together closely to implement it, including through the measures financed using the Cooperative Threat Reduction (CTR) legislation sponsored by Senators Sam Nunn and Richard Lugar. CTR was a conceptual breakthrough because previously states were responsible for implementing the obligations that they took on in treaties using their own technical and financial resources. Under CTR, it was established that where an objective was shared, states could also pool their knowledge and money to reach the desirable end-state as quickly as possible. In 1996, the UN General Assembly adopted the Comprehensive Test Ban Treaty (CTBT). In 1997, the IAEA Board of Governors approved the Protocol Additional to Safeguards Agreements, granting the Agency, complementary inspection authority in countries that adopt it.

In the non-nuclear field, in 1990, the Treaty on Conventional Armed Forces in Europe (CFE Treaty) was signed and during the 1990s, hundreds of thousands of heavy weapons were being destroyed in Europe, in a process under full transparency and intrusive verification. In 1992, the UN General Assembly adopted the Chemical Weapons Convention, which entered into force in 1993 and created the conditions for the destruction of roughly seventy thousand tonnes of chemical weapons. This destruction process was overseen by a dedicated body, the Organisation for the Prohibition of Chemical Weapons, ensuring full transparency and intrusive verification.

---

[4] 2000 Review Conference of the Parties to the Treaty on the Non-Proliferation of Nuclear Weapons, Final Document, Volume I, Part I, *Review of the operation of the Treaty, taking into account the decisions and the resolution adopted by the 1995 Review and Extension Conference*, UN document NPT/CONF.2000/28 (Parts I and II), New York, 2000.

[5] Decision 2, *Principles and Objectives for Nuclear Non-Proliferation and Disarmament*, UN document NPT/CONF.1995/32 (Part I), Annex.

In the same period, Iraq, a country that sought a range of illegal nuclear and biological weapons and both built and used an arsenal of chemical weapons, was disarmed under the legal authority of the United Nations, with specialised bodies playing a central role.

In spite of these successes, the period leading up to the 2000 Review Conference was also one in which some of the key political and strategic factors that underpinned progress in arms control, were under severe strain. The relationship in the security field between Russia and the United States was deteriorating, not in the least because of changing domestic political conditions in both countries. The domestic reaction to agreements reached between President Bill Clinton and President Boris Yeltsin in 1997 intended to create the conditions for further arms reductions and illustrated how brittle the relationship had become over matters that are still unresolved— the appropriate size of the US military footprint in Europe and the role of anti-ballistic missile defences.

Outside the most important bilateral relationship, seen from the perspective of arms control, there were other events that contributed to the feeling that arms control may have proved its worth in the immediate transition from the Cold War but had more limited scope in other areas. In 1998, North Korea tested a medium-range ballistic missile by firing it over the territory of Japan without warning or consultation and India and Pakistan both conducted nuclear weapon tests, bringing their latent nuclear weapon arsenals into the open.

These events provided evidence that the existing multilateral treaties were not sufficient. For some, the conclusion was that if states did not sign treaties in good faith then new and stronger measures were badly needed to shore up arms control gains. However, for others, these developments were signals that arms control was an unreliable instrument in the national security policy and that investment in national military capabilities could not be neglected.

Non-proliferation

Turning to the issue of non-proliferation, there also, it has been a mixed picture in the recent past. The illegal nuclear weapons program in Libya was both revealed and dismantled peacefully shortly after the international network conducting illicit trafficking in very proliferation-sensitive equipment and technology was made public and disrupted. The fact that Iraq had been successfully disarmed under United Nations auspices was revealed in the aftermath of a war that also had many negative consequences, undermining the cohesiveness of even the strong international partnerships such as NATO and unleashing new rounds of instability and conflict in the Middle East and beyond.

At the same time, the official and non-governmental communities concerned about the risk of proliferation have had to work harder to convince both state and non-state audiences that non-proliferation is indeed a real security priority after the misuse of intelligence in the run up to the Iraq War. Partly as a result of the need to restore solidarity, new players have also entered the non-proliferation field in the past decade. The view is increasingly taking hold that the non-proliferation regime is not synonymous with the NPT, but is rather what John Carlson has called a series of 'complex interacting and mutually reinforcing elements'.

In recent years, the G8 group of industrialised states has validated itself as a significant part of the international non-proliferation and counter-terrorism architecture and the discussions among the group of national directors of non-proliferation policy that meet under G8 auspices help inform national decision making. A decade ago, at their summit in Kananaskis, Canada in 2002, the G8 leaders agreed on a set of six principles to prevent terrorists, or those that harbour them, from gaining access to weapons or materials of mass destruction, without detracting from the importance of multilateral approaches, based on the consent of all parties—in fact the first of the Kananaskis principles was to 'promote the adoption, universalisation, full implementation and, where necessary, strengthening of multilateral treaties and other international instruments whose aim is to prevent the proliferation or illicit acquisition' of weapons or materials of mass destruction.

The European Union elaborated its *Strategy against the proliferation of materials and weapons of mass destruction* in December 2003 and over the past 10 years, the EU has underlined that proliferation was a priority threat and also developed programs and instruments to implement its policies. Other regional bodies in Africa, Asia and Latin America have also emphasised their positive engagement with the issue, including the development of innovative approaches (such as the Argentine–Brazilian Agency for Accounting and Control of Nuclear Materials (ABACC)) and the bringing into being of nuclear weapon-free zones. These actions have reinforced and supplemented the political and legal norms contained in the NPT, to the point where very few countries in the world could now be said to challenge them openly.

Special mention should be made of the changing balance in the respective role played by the UN Security Council in arms control vis-à-vis multilateral forums. The Security Council has acted as a political driver. In September 2009, the Council meeting of Heads of State focussed specifically on nuclear issues. This was the first to be chaired by the US President and led to the unanimous adoption of Resolution 1887. The Security Council has also acted as a legislator in the arms control field. Security Council Resolution 1540, adopted in April 2004, requires Member States to enact domestic legislation to strengthen their non-proliferation capacities, including the use of criminal law. In a series of country-specific resolutions focussed on Iran and North Korea, the Security Council has required Member States to apply restrictive measures and sanctions in an effort to block the flow of specified items into and out of those countries and to try and bring about a change in policy on nuclear matters in Tehran and Pyongyang.

The International Atomic Energy Agency (IAEA) has been the vanguard of the effort to increase nuclear transparency worldwide, through a combination of enhanced legal authority, greater requirements for disclosure by states with nuclear programs and a stronger emphasis on using existing authority (such as the right to conduct special inspections and the right of access to the UN Security Council). Achieving this greater transparency by strengthening the nuclear safeguards system depends critically on the process of concluding and bringing into force additional protocols to the safeguards agreements between IAEA and its member states, based on the Model Additional Protocol agreed on, in 1997.

As of October 2011, 111 states as well as EURATOM have additional protocols in force. However, the list of states where the additional protocol is not yet in force includes not only Iran and North Korea but also many others that are of considerable interest from a non-proliferation perspective.

There has also been a gradual recognition that modern and effective national export controls are needed to implement non-proliferation commitments. The Nuclear Suppliers Group, where states cooperate informally to enhance the effectiveness of national controls, has recognised the need to strengthen controls over a particularly sensitive item in the civilian nuclear fuel cycle. Through, among other things, the NSG discussions, it is now better understood that export controls must include not only nuclear material but also a wide range of 'dual-use' commodities and technologies that can contribute to a program of concern. Through the development of the Proliferation Security Initiative, states have recognised that the legal authority to interdict goods or block the provision of services is needed all along the supply chain, not only at the point of export. They have also given notice of their intention to strengthen the enforcement of those rules, both nationally and through enhanced international cooperation, by participating in PSI.

There have been periodic reminders of the vulnerability of the non-proliferation regime, including the failure to make substantive progress on several nuclear issues in the Middle East, primarily the widespread belief that Israel possesses a significant quantity of nuclear weapons and the serious concerns raised by some aspects of Iran's nuclear program. Controversy over Iran's civilian nuclear program and the serious questions it raises has also served as a reminder of the fact that the larger issue of how to control effectively, sensitive dual-use technologies that can be diverted from peaceful uses, is not only unresolved but may also grow in importance.

In summary, in spite of recent achievements, there is still a widespread uncertainty about the long-term durability of both disarmament measures and what has been achieved in blocking the emergence of new nuclear-armed states and a degree of concern that past achievements might be rolled back.

Underlying dynamics and remedies

The previous sections have outlined what has been a largely technical approach to reducing the role of nuclear weapons in international relations. However, it is worth reflecting on the underlying political and military dynamics that help shape the arms control environment.

Efforts to define and apply essentially constructive uses of conventional armed forces and the controversies that have sprung up around them have been close to the top of our minds, following the military intervention in Libya. During the Cold War, the major powers laid a heavy emphasis on avoiding the use of force, at least in part, because of the deployment of nuclear weapons on either side of the Cold War divide and the adoption of a strategy of nuclear deterrence. A simple equation can be used to describe the dampening effect that nuclear weapons had on the appetite for conflict among major powers: unrestricted conflict + nuclear weapons = holocaust.

The risk that any conflict would escalate to the use of nuclear weapons was a factor that the most senior decision makers in the major powers were constantly aware of. These leaders (who already tended to be risk averse for the most part) not only had a strong incentive to be cautious in their handling of direct bilateral crises, they also had good reason to restrain the actions of their client states.

It was rare for the main institutions (particularly, the United Nations) to play a key role in crisis management, which tended to be channeled through bilateral contact between the United States and the Soviet Union as the leaders of the two adversarial blocs whose confrontation was the dominant feature of the international system. Attitudes to armed conflict were conditioned by the bipolar competition rather than local factors and, as a result, once one superpower became engaged in a particular crisis, its rival had little choice but to join in.

In the first decade after the end of the Cold War, the approach towards the use of force to achieve positive results was mainly thought of as cooperation under the auspices of the United Nations, with the coalition effort to reverse Iraqi aggression against Kuwait, perhaps the high point of that cooperative spirit. In January 1999, the NATO Council decided that the Alliance could carry out air strikes against targets in Serbia to compel compliance with existing decisions and to help bring about the conditions for a political settlement.

The decisions taken at the end of the 1990s were also in line with another post-Cold War tendency, namely to see force, less as an instrument to be applied in conflicts among states and more as an instrument that could target what was considered to be inappropriate behaviour—whether by the leaders of states or subsequently non-state groups considered to present a threat serious enough to require a military response.

The 1999 NATO decision, enacted over the strong objections of Russia and China, can perhaps be seen as the moment where the emerging consensus that cooperation under the UN Security Council was the main executive mechanism for managing international conflict, was lost. Subsequently, the shift away from cooperation and consensus about the use of force for ostensibly constructive purposes, gathered momentum, culminating in the war in Iraq in 2003, which proved to be so divisive that it became a near death experience for NATO.

The move away from cooperation reinforced the voices of those who insist nuclear weapons still play a useful role as a hedge against any future deterioration in relations among the major powers. Other countries had perhaps already drawn their own conclusion that if nuclear weapons in the hands of a regime, like the one in Pyongyang, allowed an essentially weak player to paralyse much stronger players by nuclear threats, then the benefits from investing in them would outweigh any negative consequences.

The result is that big powers and small powers, established nuclear states and potential proliferators today are still convinced that having nuclear weapons can help to solve the underlying challenge of insecurity, in spite of the compelling evidence that it cannot. At best it can produce a long, costly and dangerous stalemate, like the Cold War or the current India-Pakistan relationship. In other cases, the risk that new nuclear weapon capabilities might appear, whether in new hands or old hands, produces anxieties and counter-reactions that make the overall security situation worse.

Where subjective visions of shifts in relative power take hold over strategic elites, even democratic countries begin to elaborate the wrong remedies to new nuclear threats. If states become concerned that the relative value of their military power is being undermined, we have seen how quickly they can fall into a 'use or lose' mentality where emerging dangers must be crushed before it is too late.

The European Union's strategy against WMD was largely formed with a view to counter-balancing this way of thinking, with the idea that the best solution to the problem of nuclear weapons is that countries should no longer feel that they need them. This is not so much of a vague and idealistic idea as it sounds but can actually help countries make detailed choices in the way they approach nuclear-related problems. For instance, if they accept that security is one Iranian motive for pursuing sensitive nuclear capabilities, it should be clear that threatening to attack Iran or overthrow their regime can only make things worse from a proliferation perspective.

It also follows that those that are seen as problem states will never be content to live with solutions that suit all but leave them weaker and more exposed. So, changing their security perceptions and behaviour for the long term must be based on positive prospects and incentives as well as warnings and sanctions.

These points are corroborated by past cases of 'de-nuclearisation', when states who pulled back from nuclear weapons all did so at a time when they were shifting the emphasis of their national policy to seek the political and economic benefits of participation and integration into wider international processes. By contrast, the approach of using coercive tools to bring about de-proliferation might produce durable results in the country where it is applied, but it cannot generate momentum for wider changes through the power of positive emulation. On the contrary, it is likely to stimulate resistance in countries that consider their programs likely future targets and entrench policies, based on deception and concealment. Therefore the formula is known; one just needs to have an open mind and be united enough to apply it in the new way that is needed for each case.

Pathways to nuclear disarmament

From this, five observations arise, about how a more permissive environment for denuclearisation might be created and one that can offer pathways forward. First, uncertainty is increased because the current system of rules governing the legitimate application of force is no longer adequate in contemporary conditions. In the absence of understandable and widely accepted guidelines, the cases where force is used come to be seen as ad hoc, unpredictable and politically driven. As long as states are uncertain about which actions will trigger a military response and which will not, they are likely to seek not only reassurance but also insurance against contingencies where they may find themselves subject to pressure or coercion. Establishing a modern, rule-based framework for the legitimate use of force in the non-nuclear security environment is a first precondition for disarmament.

Second, if major powers are concerned that a peer may see force as a legitimate instrument that can be used to address disagreements, they are likely to maintain a hedge in the form of nuclear weapons. The lack of agreed rules has been exacerbated by the increased tendency of states and groups of states to define and implement what they regard as constructive uses of military force. Organising the relations between major powers in ways that minimise the risk of war is therefore the second precondition for progress towards disarmament.

Third, there is widespread agreement on the normative framework in place related to nuclear, biological and chemical weapons today and the vast majority of states comply with their obligations voluntarily and in full. A handful of states have decided not to participate in the existing framework, but according to their declaratory policies, these states have no objection in principle to irreversible disarmament, provided that it is robust and comprehensive.

A second category of deviant states are more problematic in that there are cases of deliberate and systematic violation of legal undertakings, given in apparent good faith. This represents the greatest threat to irreversible disarmament because such activities undermine the cooperation between states in compliance with mutual reassurance. Managing relations with the small group of states in which there is low confidence regarding their respect for nuclear, biological and chemical weapon-related arms control is the third precondition for progress towards disarmament.

Fourth, experience suggests that the most effective international response to such cases has been the continuous and direct engagement of the UN Security Council, using all the instruments and authority at its disposal. In contrast, indirect engagement—in effect delegating authority and encouraging Member States to find solutions to the problem—has been less successful. The successful disarmament of Iraq in the 1990s, through direct action, under a UN umbrella and the failure (so far) to disarm North Korea through a more indirect method are the clearest examples of the two approaches.

There was a belief, in the wake of the Cold War, that standing security institutions could be more effectively replaced by ad hoc coalitions of states. The failures of this approach in practice have only reinforced recognition that standing institutions are needed not only to marshal resources effectively but also to provide continuity and sustain engagement in the complex tasks of enforcing, keeping and building peace.

The UN Security Council remains the forum where political understanding can be hammered out among major powers and then, if their national perspectives can be reconciled, codified in decisions that are published, affording a degree of transparency. There is little doubt that the UN Security Council could be improved, but a fundamental reform of the Security Council has so far proved impossible and other ways need to be found to maintain its relevance and effectiveness.

The participation of the current batch of contemporary major powers in the UN Security Council cannot be sustained, as non-permanent members cannot be immediately re-elected after a two-year term. The benefits of the recent Security Council configurations risk getting lost. Flexible ways need to be found to sustain a continuous engagement with the new major powers; both regarding what constitutes a threat to international peace and security and in crafting a response.

Fifth, one country—the United States—has been central to efforts to address security problems both regionally and globally. The US is the only country that has the combination of aspiration, authority, resources, power and reach to implement a truly global, foreign and security policy. While the role of the United States is critical, the US is clearly entering a period of reflection and evaluation as the implications of two decades of global leadership are assessed. In a period of reflection, the temptation to seek a temporary disengagement from external matters is likely to grow. The voices of those who are ambivalent about the degree to which the United States should embrace multilateralism are likely to make themselves heard.

It is vital for the international community to emphasise to the United States, the mutual advantages of its continued leadership. However, it is not just the United States, but all of the main centres of power that are reflecting on the efficiency of current systems of national, regional and international governance, in light of the scale and nature of the security problems facing their citizens. This is the time for joint reflection, not disengagement and the time for open-minded discussion regarding the best solutions to identified problems.

The United States is not only the inventor of nuclear weapons and one of the main possessor states, it is also the place where most of the research and development of other, more novel, military technologies currently takes place. The scale of investment in the military sector by the United States and its broad scope, differentiates it from other states and is inevitably a key factor taken into account by other countries. Engaging the USA in the international system on the basis of responsible leadership within a common framework is therefore a fifth precondition for disarmament.

Nuclear Disarmament: Perspectives from the IAEA

Sheel Kant Sharma

For several short periods throughout the nuclear age, prospects for nuclear arms control and nuclear disarmament appeared to be at hand but proved largely elusive. However, the hesitant revival in the present period has been unprecedented. For the first time since 1956, the US strategic weapons count has gone below 2000 to 1968 at the end of 2009 and appears irreversible. It is for the first time since the First Special session of UNGA devoted to disarmament (1978) that all nuclear weapon states are, for whatever it is worth, accepting the elimination of nuclear weapons as a goal and if one goes by the final document of the last NPT Review Conference in 2010, the non-nuclear weapon states now have a political commitment from the NWS for elimination. The UN Secretary General, in his five point proposal in 2008, visualised a comprehensive process of nuclear disarmament when he spoke of "A new convention or a set of mutually reinforcinginstruments to eliminate nuclear weapons, backed by strong verification; a UN summit on nuclear disarmament; rooting nuclear Disarmament in legal obligations; requiring nuclear weapons states to publish information about what they are doing to fulfil their Disarmament obligations and; limiting missiles, space weapons, and Conventional arms."

Likewise, the NPT Rev Con in 2010 called on "all nuclear weapons states to undertake concrete disarmament efforts and affirms that all states need to make special efforts to establish the necessary framework to achieve and maintain a world without nuclear weapons". The summits in Prague and Washington Summit in 2010 also showed a change in outlook and traction towards this elusive goal.

The seminal essays on the subject by the Cold War hardliners, Kissinger, Nunn, Perry, and Shultz (Jan 2007, Oct 2008, March 2010) point to precarious fault lines in the deterrent theories which have sustained the nuclear arms race, over the decades. They have actually suggested steps as to how to go about the elimination of nuclear weapons. There is admission today of contingencies, resulting in weakness or failure or irrelevance of the MAD doctrine, particularly due to terrorism. The review made earlier this year of India's official Action Plan of 1988 for a nuclear weapon free world, reaffirms commitment to elimination through systematic steps within a set timeline. The net impact of these initiatives can be seen diminishing not only the salience of nuclear weapons but also the pre-disposition of nuclear weapon states to deploy them. Moreover, what is common to all these important documents is insistence on a process or a framework or a plan to reach the goal.

The institutional requirements for such a systematic process, whenever it became possible, would be stupendous. Naturally, looking at existing machinery would make sense. It is of utmost importance here to note that the overarching moral and humanitarian imperative for nuclear disarmament inescapably gives way to security considerations of states, once negotiations or even pre-negotiations commence – even the essays of the Four have gradually shown due regard for maintenance of security. Recent developments indicate that in a whole range of priorities for a multilateral agenda in any field, be that economy, climate change or nuclear issues; difficulties abound in translating the moral imperative into a political imperative globally – much less any legal compact. However, as those campaigning for elimination wait for an opportunity, preparation for practical aspects concerning the various steps, should begin.

Broadly, two kinds of multilateral and bilateral frameworks might be necessary: those for negotiations for step by step arms reduction and those for compliance and verification. (Example: CD negotiated CW Convention, which is implemented by OPCW; CD negotiated the CTBT which the CTBTO strives to implement).

During the Cold War decades, US and Soviet Union had made some progress in negotiated nuclear arms control (SALT, ABM, Threshold Test Ban) and reductions (START, INF) while other NWS merely gave out qualified declarations to reassure the world about their intentions to pursue nuclear disarmament and cessation of nuclear arms race under certain conditions. The START process continued even after the Cold War, albeit less reassuringly, till the entry into force of the New START treaty.

This is broadly the setting in which one can situate a perspective from the IAEA. It is true that in the institutional arrangements required in the aforementioned bilateral or trilateral process, the IAEA did not figure at all but the Nobel Peace Prize citation for IAEA and its DG in 2005 has very significant words:

"...the International Atomic Energy Agency (IAEA) and its Director General, Mohamed ElBaradei, for their efforts to prevent nuclear energy from being used for military purposes and to ensure that nuclear energy for peaceful purposes is used in the safest possible way."

"At a time when the threat of nuclear arms is again increasing, the Norwegian Nobel Committee wishes to underline that this threat must be met through the broadest possible international cooperation. "

"At a time when disarmament efforts appear deadlocked, when there is a danger that nuclear arms will spread both to states and to terrorist groups, and when nuclear power again appears to be playing an increasingly significant role, IAEA's work is of incalculable importance."(why separate quotes?)

This principle finds its clearest expression today in the work of the IAEA and its Director General. In the nuclear non-proliferation regime, it is the IAEA which controls and verifies, under given legal instruments, that nuclear energy is not misused for military purposes, and the Director General has stood out as an unafraid advocate of new measures to strengthen that regime. The above citation, when seen side by side with the original and historic "Atoms for Peace" speech of President Eisenhower's in 1953, provides the full view of IAEA's wingspan as it has grown over the past sixty years. The essential point of the "Atoms for Peace" speech was that both the benefits and the dangers posed to international security by nuclear science must be addressed by the comity of nations in a cooperative way. The IAEA was set up in 1957 with this basic tenet. It went through ups and down during the Cold War decades and was skewed to such an extent that the label of nuclear watchdog got stuck to it. The Nobel Prize and the citation sought to restore the balance. The former DG, ElBaradei ,having ceaselessly worked with that balance in sight, left the Agency in pretty good shape for his successor.

How relevant are these asides to the perspective of nuclear disarmament? It is a fact that in none of the nuclear disarmament milestones so far, was the IAEA legally involved. The NPT was the solitary exception where central responsibility was placed in the IAEA for safeguards implementation. Critics have argued, however, that the NPT is not a nuclear disarmament measure.

The safeguards edifice was founded upon the 1957 IAEA Statute which provided the legal framework of IAEA's activities for cooperation in nuclear science and technology, subject to acceptance of safeguards by states concerned. This, however, progressed on an entirely different course in the wake of the NPT related safeguards or comprehensive safeguards which today form an accepted canon of global disarmament. At the core of the entire safeguards corpus of the IAEA, is the cooperative commitment to enforce accounting and control of nuclear materials as well as inspections and monitoring of nuclear facilities to rule out diversion for military purpose.

The role of IAEA, thus will remain integral to any multilateral process of nuclear disarmament. The move to have a treaty banning production of fissile material also flows from this core constituent of nuclear disarmament and though negotiations of FMCT remains deadlocked in CD. Any future treaty would have to draw upon safeguards framework nurtured and developed by the IAEA.

It is useful to see the full spectrum of IAEA's safeguards related work, well over the past six decades which has comprised:

- Materials Accounting and control and monitoring of nuclear facilities in non nuclear weapon states under more or less standard agreements (Infcirc 66, Infcirc 149, model Additional Protocol Infcirc 540)

- Materials accounting and monitoring of voluntarily offered facilities in NWS, in a framework of varying legal instruments covering each of the NPT NWS

- Special arrangements with regional safeguards systems such as EURATOM or ABAC,

- Arrangements with States adhering to NWFZ in Africa, Latin America, South East Asia, South Pacific

- Trilateral Arrangement with USA and Russian Federation about disposal of dismantled warheads from the ex- Soviet states of Belarus, Kazakhstan and Ukraine

- Dismantling of the nuclear facilities of Iraq after 1991 Gulf War under UNSC 687 and its various sequels

- Application of safeguards on South Africa's nuclear facilities to verify its unilateral nuclear disarmament after the end of apartheid; and

- India specific safeguards agreement following the Indo-US nuclear agreement.

The activities mentioned above are extensive in detail and implementation. The underlying framework of legal instruments for each of them have evolved over the years, particularly since the end of the cold war, progressively tightening inspections, monitoring, analysis and engagement with authorities of States placed under safeguards. The purpose of safeguards is to inspire confidence among parties to treaties like NPT, or NWFZ or bilateral agreements of States with IAEA about adherence to safeguards obligations for declared non diversion of nuclear material and facilities from civil to military use. In this manner, the IAEA multilaterally enforces control on nuclear facilities and material placed under safeguards.

In addition, after Iraq's clandestine nuclear weapon program came to light before the first Gulf War, the IAEA played an exceptional role with a mandate from its Board of Governors; which in turn was backstopped by the experience of UNSCOM in implementing UNSC resolution 687. This mandate was frankly tantamount to one for drafting a sequel to NPT to plug a major lacuna, that is, the possibility of a state party to NPT pursuing a hidden weapons program, unbeknown to the IAEA, by simply not declaring it. Through strengthened safeguards under the so called 93 +2 process and subsequently, the model additional protocol to NPT type safeguards agreements, the IAEA virtually drafted a NPT II without subjecting the states to long winded negotiations under the CD. In that sense, it served tacitly as a negotiating forum through the Committee 24 which was set up by the Board of Governors in mid-nineties. The Model additional Protocol is in force in more than 100 countries, even though notable exceptions remain in the Middle East. The additional Protocol ensures that all declared or undeclared activities in States Party to NPT are under IAEA's safeguards system.

The entire experience of tracking Iran's nuclear program, since 2003, is an important facet of IAEA's work in progress. On the other hand, the severe limitations in verifying North Korea's nuclear program reveal another serious drawback.

The book, *The Age of Deception* by Mohamed Elbaradei pithily describes these diverse experiences of IAEA in lucid detail. ElBaradei commends IAEA's role in nuclear diplomacy comprising "nearly half a century of painstaking labour by committed scientists, lawyers, inspectors, and public servants from every continent". He calls nuclear diplomacy "a hands-on-discipline requiring direct engagement, restraint and long-term commitment."

The diverse activities of IAEA have aimed at creating a modicum of confidence in the multilateral system, but this confidence level will need to multiply manifold in the event of a truly multilateral process of nuclear disarmament being visualised. The IAEA, to borrow a common expression from nuclear fuel cycle, covers the *back end*, as it were, of a nuclear disarmament process the *front end* of which would have to consist of drastic reductions in largest stockpiles of nuclear weapons, restraint or prohibition of their use, global reductions in weapons of all nuclear weapon states and possibly some security undertakings.

Realistically, even after steps are taken on the *front end*, the lurking security threats may not diminish but might even increase; particularly in the present day apprehensions about terrorists' access to nuclear weapons. Hence a thorough system of control on all nuclear material for weapons use and monitoring of facilities becomes necessary, plus additional steps by common global consent to provide for security of the facilities and nuclear material. Both the *front end* and the *back end* would thus need to go hand in hand.

Viewing in some detail, the existing core competence of IAEA through case studies of Iraq, South Africa, the former Soviet states of Ukraine, Belarus and Kazakhstan, North Korea, Iran and what has been slickly called the nuclear Wal-Mart run by Kader Khan & Co., Iraq was discovered to have cheated the NPT parties by not declaring its weapons program, keeping it hidden from IAEA inspections under the NPT safeguards (INFCIRC 149). The Security Council took the unprecedented step of prescribing Iraq's comprehensive disarmament through the resolution 687, covering inter alia missiles, nuclear facilities developing enrichment, reprocessing as well as those connected with other weapons of mass destruction. The IAEA took charge of implementing nuclear part of 687.

In the years 1991-2000, the IAEA brought about disarmament of Iraq's nuclear program - the military dimension of which was uncovered in September 1991 by IAEA inspectors in central Baghdad. In this process, there were many obstacles which are narrated by ElBaradei in his book. The mandate of 687 was resisted by the Iraqi establishment by concealment, denial and refusal to admit inspectors. Since force was used by the US-led coalition, that threat was often used to prevail over the Iraqi resistance but eventually it was the engagement of the IAEA senior staff with Iraqi government that allowed tracking the trajectory of Iraqi nuclear program, since its onset in 1982; gaining control of any enriched uranium in Iraq's possession and destroying the enrichment and reprocessing equipment fully. As years passed, the UNSCOM got into problems due to the heavy handed approach of the US and UK and the clampdown of Iraqi air space (no-fly-zones) and repeated strikes on Iraqi targets. While this led to expulsion of UNSCOM teams from Iraq and suspension of even IAEA's work, the IAEA inspectors had secured detailed knowledge of the Iraqi nuclear program. This was in the background when ElBaradei eventually stated; in the face of persistent US and UK claims before the UNSC in 2003; that Iraq did not have a nuclear weapons program.

This process of disarmament was no doubt akin to disarmament of the vanquished rather than a cooperative voluntarily negotiated process. However, the experience of working out the tracking, control and destruction was of great value. It could be contrasted with the verification of South Africa's voluntarily offered disarmament of nuclear capability of the apartheid regime and placing of resulting peaceful facilities, material etc. under full scope safeguards.

The lesser known and advertised part of IAEA's quiet work concerns the three nuclear states which emerged out of Soviet collapse in 1991. These states had nuclear material, facilities and scientists inherited from the Soviet weapons complex. They all joined NPT as non-nuclear weapon states but the task of ensuring their compliance and bringing their facilities under full scope safeguards was a tedious and time consuming one. There were threats of nuclear smuggling from these states as well as from Russia itself - to deal with which a multilateral approach was also desirable, apart from the bilateral US approaches with the help of Russia and other European states. The IAEA gained experience as it set about creating state systems of accounting and controls in these states and bringing about security and physical protection of their nuclear facilities and material. This too can figure in the general rubric of disarmament, albeit through ad hoc and contingency measures.

The bomb grade plutonium and enriched uranium made available through the process was put to a trilateral arrangement of disposal among US, Russia and the IAEA. It required blending down the fissile material and burning it through MOX fuel. The pathways traversed in this entire exercise would be germane to a nuclear disarmament agreement of the future. Its daunting dimension can be gauged by the fact that the expected blending and downgrading of weapons usable nuclear material has a long and expensive gestation period; the US facilities where MOX fuel would be burnt have announced commencement only in recent years.

The DPRK experience for the IAEA was different in that DPRK never really put in force NPT safeguards: its mandatory initial declaration to IAEA after formal ratification of its safeguards agreement in 1992 was far from credible. To the questions put by the IAEA, they presented a tissue of false explanations and made attempts at concealment about plutonium experiments, reprocessing etc. The IAEA inspectors detected discrepancies in DPRK's declarations about the plutonium it possessed and its activities about reprocessing. However, DPRK denied and negotiated hard for every bit of clarification sought by IAEA teams, resisted access and even misled inspectors. It walked out of the NPT owing to IAEA's persistent demand for inspections and transmission of DPRK's file to the UN Security Council. DPRK was persuaded to return through the Framework Agreement of 1994, negotiated by Jimmy Carter, but only partially. IAEA's role was confined to monitoring the freeze in the plutonium production reactor at Yongbyon and associated reprocessing - without any access to its past activities or activities in other sites where facilities were under construction. DPRK was neither fully in nor out of NPT but the framework agreement envisaged its return to NPT through a set of actions and reciprocal actions underwritten by US, Japan, China and Russia. The IAEA engagement with DPRK made the world wise about its intentions but China's insistence on dialogue and restraint to resolve outstanding issues prevented the Security Council from taking any harsh measures – say, as was done for Iraq. The North Koreans quit the IAEA as the Agency sought (in vain) special inspections, through specially convened meetings of its board of governors and references to Security Council.

The present situation about North Korea has challenges for the global nonproliferation regime, not only due to its nuclear testing in 2006 and 2009 and threats of repeating it, but also due to its role in transfer of missile and technology to potential violators in sync with the Kader Khan network of a global Wal-Mart, which too has been pursued by the IAEA during the past two decades of on and off engagement with DPRK. The six power engagements on North Korea have been on and off over the past decade; arguably exploited by Pyongyang for further build up. As IAEA remains out of North Korea since April 2009, information about its activities can come only from national intelligence sources of the member states.

Iran's case is the most serious one as it carries, in troubling ways, the risk of escalation of conflict in the Middle East. IAEA remains engaged in Iran substantially and its reports since 2003 constitute a detailed study of how the multilateral process is coming to grips with the most serious challenge to the existing non-proliferation order. Iran's insistence on its program being peaceful, its continuation of enrichment at more than one locations at a determined pace, with increasing sophistication and a number of associate activities have raised questions. The IAEA has systematically tried to address these questions and outstanding issues through engagement with Iran. Iran in turn has not severed its engagement with IAEA so far despite, what it considers unacceptable, grave provocations such as the referral to UNSC and the sanctions and prohibitions imposed on it. During the past six years, the situation on ground has moved in a manner which erodes confidence in multilateral diplomacy to resolve the Iran imbroglio – ElBaradei, in his book, gives an impassioned plea for more room for diplomacy and cautions against threats of use of force or crippling sanctions. At the outset, possibilities of diplomatic solutions are not ruled out since proposals to break the deadlock keep coming.

The stalemate essentially comprises demands on Iran to suspend its enrichment activities and fully engage with the IAEA through formal adherence to the Additional Protocol to settle all outstanding questions about the exclusively peaceful nature of its program. Iran refuses to allow IAEA anything beyond the NPT safeguards agreement of 1974 and maintains that enrichment is its right under the NPT since it is required for its nuclear power plants, existing and planned. Iran also would like to engage with the US and European states under a 5 party or 5+1 party dialogue but demands closure of the IAEA file on it and revocation of Security Council actions against it.

Israel fears that dialogue would be Iran's way of biding time till it perfects it's already advanced weapons related work, including production of HEU. The right wing in US domestic politics sympathises with Israel and accuses President Obama of being weak-kneed. Presidential elections next year would preclude any soft line by US on Iran while global economic crisis, rise of China and weakening of US economy and support of Russia and China has emboldened Iran to dig its heels.

Such a situation would be extremely critical for any disarmament measure or process of the future. Yet the good sense of IAEA's continued engagement provides hope for multilateralism in disarmament. If this breaks down it would take much more violence and penitence before the world can return to sanity in approaching the topic of nuclear disarmament.

It is also true that constant highlights on Iran's alleged nuclear weapon program has led to IAEA's safeguards inspection and analyses, pushing the envelope to examine activities about the military dimension of nuclear and missile programs. The IAEA's reports on Iran have progressively delved into these aspects as part of outstanding issues – much to Iran's strong chagrin and rejection. However, the resolution of the Iran imbroglio, through diplomatic engagement, may strengthen IAEA for the future. Failure of diplomacy on the other hand may mean larger failures on multiple fronts and serious setback to IAEA.

Elimination of nuclear weapons and a systematic process of nuclear disarmament would have to be anchored on a paradigm of security which is multilaterally accepted. This, in turn, demands strong and alert institutions, multilaterally, regionally and also nationally. The last, because of Kader Khan's kind of willing suspension of disbelief would hardly work. The IAEA can certainly qualify to be among such institutions; provided that the doubts and apprehensions about Iran's nuclear posture could be satisfactorily resolved.

In conclusion, following the example of pre-negotiation work on the two existing disarmament treaties, namely, the CWC and CTBT, similar early work should commence under the broad IAEA auspices to devise the steps for nuclear disarmament as compatible to the IAEA's Statute, its core competence and its accumulated experience in nuclear diplomacy for almost six decades. To begin with, an intergovernmental expert group should be convened by the Board of Governors to brainstorm about implications of, and prospects opened by, recent US-Russia strategic arms reductions, the nuclear security summits and ideas espoused by a whole host of global initiatives for nuclear disarmament. The expert group could be asked to examine how the best use can be made of IAEA, in the overall context of a *set of mutually reinforcing* steps or measures that figure in the UN Secretary General's proposal as also in other eminent global initiatives.

China & Nuclear Disarmament

Alexander Kolbin

Since the 2008 article by the Four Wise Men, calling for a resurrection of the idea of nuclear zero[1], there has been a renaissance of many aspects of disarmament. For a variety of reasons, many of them fell by the wayside in the early 2000s. But in the spring of 2009, Barack Obama became the first US president to make nuclear zero part of the official discourse of American foreign policy. In April 2010, the United States hosted the first Nuclear Security Summit. The United States and Russia then signed the New START treaty in Prague, which entered into force in February 2011. And in May 2010, New York hosted the NPT Review Conference which produced the Plan of Action on nuclear disarmament and non-proliferation.

The period from 2012 to 2020 could become even more important for nuclear disarmament than the previous decade. Two more NPT review conferences shall be held. The 2012 schedule includes a conference on setting up a WMD-free zone in the Middle East and another Nuclear Security Summit in South Korea. By 2020, the United States is expected to complete all three phases of the deployment of the European segment of its global missile defence system[2]. In 2018, it will launch full-scale deployment of the advanced SM-3 Block IIA interceptors in the Asia Pacific segment of the system.[3] Finally, it is quite likely that the implementation

---

[1] Shultz P., Perry W., Kissinger G., Nunn S., "Toward a Nuclear Free World", *Wall Street Journal*, January 15, 2008, http://online.wsj.com/article/SB120036422673589947.html?mod=opinion_main_commentaries (Retrieved on July 12, 2011).

[2] *For detailed description of the phased adaptive approach to the deployment of the Euro-Atlantic segment of America's global missile defence system, see:* O'Reilly, Patrick. Trans-Atlantic Missile Defence: Looking to Lisbon, *Welcome and First Keynote: 10/12/10 – Transcript, US Atlantic Council,* http://www.acus.org/event/transatlantic-missile-defence-looking-lisbon/welcome-first-keynote-transcript (Retrieved on June 30, 2011).

[3] Statement of Dr. James N. Miller, Principal Deputy Under Secretary of Defence for Policy before the House Committee, on Armed Services Subcommittee on Strategic Forces. March 2, 2011 http://armedservices.house.gov/index.cfm/files/serve?File_id=10a50d6f-ece1-475f-bb5e-00ab478aefdb (Retrieved on 14 March, 2011).

of the New START treaty will be completed by the end of this decade, and as Russian Foreign Minister Sergey Lavrov put it, the time will come for "further talks on strengthening international stability and strategic parity".[4]

Amid all these changes, China, which has not made any significant changes to its nuclear strategy for the past 40 years, may find itself in a difficult situation. China has made substantial progress in every single area of national development; it has achieved steady economic growth, rapidly advanced its research and technological capability, and has modernised its army. Many researchers have therefore come to view China as the only power that could conceivably challenge the supremacy of the United States over the coming decade. But China's impressive growth also presents many challenges to the country itself.[5] One of these challenges would be to adapt China's nuclear strategy to its breakneck rate of growth and to the emergence of a new *strategic environment* which the country will inevitably have to deal with by the end of this decade.

As part of the new nuclear disarmament agenda, in recent years, China has been facing growing calls to engage more actively and constructively in the process of achieving a world free of nuclear weapons. But is Beijing ready for this? And will it be ready any time soon? This chapter discusses the most dangerous challenges China's nuclear strategy might face in the next decade. In the context of these challenges, it is important to consider the likelihood of progress towards a reduction of China's strategic nuclear arsenal over the next decade.

---

[4] Lavrov: discussion of global stability possible only after implementation of New START treaty. *RIA-Novosti*. January 14, 2011. http://ria.ru/politics/20110114/321524293.html (Retrieved on August 10, 2011). http://www.acus.org/event/transatlantic-missile-defence-looking-lisbon/welcome-first-keynote-transcript (Retrieved on June 30, 2011).

[5] One interesting source is the "Domestic Trends in the United States, China and Iran" analysis prepared in 2008 for the RAND Corporation by a group of US researchers. The paper names 2020 as the year when "China will enter a 'perfect storm' of economic, environmental, and social problems, largely of its own making. In the next 10–15 years, while trying to grow and transform its economy, China will confront the intertwined problems of premature depletion of its energy resources, faltering economic growth, inadequate provisions for its aging population and the need to remediate an extensively damaged environment. China's ability to modernise and expand its military at the same time will be constrained by these domestic challenges." The paper is available at: http://www.rand.org/pubs/monographs/2009/RAND_MG729.pdf (Retrieved on July 14, 2011).

China's 2010 National Defense White Book

In March 2011, China announced a new edition of its National Defence White Book to give the international community a better idea of its defence strategy. The first edition of the document was published in 1995. Starting from 1998, fresh editions have been published bi-annually. Experts who study China's nuclear policy have to parse each new edition for minute changes in the text. For example, based on the analysis of several editions published since 1998, experts have identified a rather significant evolution of the role and place of the terms "deterrence" and "policy of deterrence" in China's nuclear strategy.[6] In the 1998 edition, the words "policy of nuclear deterrence" had a distinctly negative connotation; they were used to describe only the nuclear strategies of other nuclear powers. In the 2000 edition, the term "deterrence" did not appear at all. And in 2006, when China first made public the key provisions of its nuclear strategy, "nuclear deterrence" was highlighted as the main task of the Second Artillery Force. One major difficulty for analysts is comparing the translations of these terms from Chinese into English to make sure that they are consistent.[7] Another common difficulty frequently pointed out by experts on China's nuclear policy is its lack of transparency; there is not enough Chinese-language information available on the subject, making the task of accurate and reliable analysis of China's nuclear strategy very difficult.[8]

The Nuclear Disarmament section of the White Book says that China has always advocated a universal ban on nuclear weapons and elimination of the existing arsenals. It stresses that the countries which possess the largest stockpiles of nuclear weapons bear special responsibility for nuclear disarmament. Beijing argues that these countries must significantly reduce their arsenals to make a complete and universal nuclear disarmament possible. Once these conditions are in place, the other nuclear powers

[6] See, for example: Liu Huaping. The Evolution of China's Nuclear Strategy and Multilateral Nuclear Disarmament. Program on Strategic Stability Evaluation (POSSE). http://www.posse.gatech.edu/sites/default/files/Liu_Jan15_Revision.pdf (Retrieved on September 1, 2011).

[7] Ibid

[8] See, for example: Perfilyev Nikita. *Transparency with Chinese Characteristics*. PacNet No. 5. 24 January, 2011, http://csis.org/files/publication/pac1105.pdf (Retrieved on August 10, 2011).

must join multilateral talks on nuclear disarmament. Also, in order to achieve the goal of universal nuclear disarmament, "the international community should develop, at an appropriate time, a viable, long-term plan with different phases, including the conclusion of a convention on the complete prohibition of nuclear weapons".[9]

Given such a statement, it is hard to imagine preconditions that would be more difficult to satisfy, thereby enabling China not to engage in nuclear disarmament for as long as it wishes. But that is not all. China also argues that in order to make a universal and complete prohibition of nuclear weapons possible, all the nations which possess nuclear weapons must refuse their policies of nuclear deterrence, based on the possibility of first use of nuclear weapons.[10] In other words, these nations must undertake a commitment "that under no circumstances will they use or threaten to use nuclear weapons against non-nuclear-weapon states or nuclear-weapon-free zones and negotiate an international legal instrument in this regard".[11]

As for Beijing's own nuclear strategy, the White Book insists that China has never tried to evade its obligations in the field of nuclear disarmament and that the country is following a transparent and responsible nuclear policy. In addition, China abides by its commitment to No First Use of nuclear weapons, whatever the circumstances. It has never deployed nuclear weapons on foreign territory and it has always exercised the utmost restraint in the development of nuclear weapons. It has never participated in any form of nuclear arms race, nor will it ever do so. It will limit its nuclear capabilities to the minimum level required for national security and it will support the efforts of non-nuclear-weapon states in establishing nuclear-weapon-free zones.[12]

Another paragraph in the White Book outlines China's stance on missile defence. Beijing believes that a global missile defence system would be harmful to international strategic balance and stability, undermine

---

[9] China's National Defence in 2010. Arms Control and Disarmament. 2011, 31 March, http://news.xinhuanet.com/english2010/china/2011-03/31/c_13806851_38.htm (Retrieved on July 2, 2011).

[10] Ibid

[11] Ibid

[12] Ibid

international and regional security and have a negative impact on nuclear disarmament. "China holds that no state should deploy overseas missile defence systems that have strategic missile defence capabilities or potential, or engage in any such international collaboration," the document reads.[13]

This position was repeated almost literally in an official statement made by China during the 2010 NPT Review Conference.[14] Indeed, China has been voicing most of these arguments (except for the objections against the deployment of a global missile defence system) ever since it acquired nuclear weapons back in 1964.[15] To summarise Beijing's official position, the main obstacles preventing China from joining the nuclear disarmament process are as follows:

- The nuclear weapon states have not yet undertaken an obligation of No First Use of nuclear weapons and to reflect this obligation on a multilateral agreement.[16]

- The United States and its allies are pressing ahead with the deployment of a global missile defence system.

- The United States and Russia, as part of their bilateral nuclear disarmament, have not yet reduced their arsenals to a level low enough to enable China to join a multilateral nuclear disarmament process.

---

[13] Ibid

[14] Implementation of the NPT. Report presented by China. 2010 NPT Review Conference, May 4, 2010, http://www.un.org/ga/search/view_doc.asp?symbol=NPT/CONF.2010/31&referer=http://www.un.org/en/conf/npt/2010/statespartiesreports.shtml&Lang=R (Retrieved on July 12, 2011).

[15] For comparison see: Statement of the Government of the People's Republic of China, 1964, 16 October, http://www.nti.org/db/china/engdocs/nucsta64.htm (Retrieved on 12 èþëÿ(the word is indecipherable) 2011); China's Instrument of Accession to the Non-proliferation Treaty. 1992, March 11, http://nuclearthreatinitiative.org/db/china/engdocs/nptdec.htm (Retrieved on July 12, 2011); for more details about the evolution of Chinese policy on nuclear nonproliferation, see: Medeiros Evan S. *Reluctant restraint: the evolution of China's nonproliferation policies and practices*, 1980 – 2004. Stanford: Stanford University Press, 2007; Zhu Mingquan., *The Evolution of China's Nuclear Nonproliferation Policy*. http://irchina.org/en/xueren/china/view.asp?id=653 (Retrieved on July 12, 2011).

[16] Detailed analysis of the possibility of such an agreement being signed is offered in Chapter 19 of the paper *Nuclear Reset: Arms Reduction and Nonproliferation*, ed. A. Arbatov and V. Dvorkin. Moscow: ROSSPEN, 2011, P. 351-366.

These are the most obvious obstacles, which China has been highlighting for several decades now. But there are other problems as well. They are less obvious, but no less important for that. These problems are preventing China from joining the nuclear disarmament process, and some of them may be intensified, depending on the political course chosen by the United States (on issues such as placing weapons in space[17] or recognizing Taiwan's independence), on the state of relations in the China-Pakistan-India triangle and on the situation in North Korea. Also, in recent years, experts have started to mention possible joint Russian-American efforts among the factors that could facilitate China's engagement in nuclear disarmament.[18]

No First Use Obligation: Role and Place in China's Nuclear Strategy

In the following, is discussed in more detail, each of the three listed obstacles. China undertook the obligation "never at any time or under any circumstances [to] be the first to use nuclear weapons" on October 16, 1964, the day it tested its first nuclear device.[19] On October 17, it proposed an international summit to discuss the possibility of introducing a comprehensive ban on nuclear weapons and eliminating all the existing nuclear arsenals. Beijing hoped that as a first step, "the summit conference

---

[17] At least until 2009, the United States actively worked on the development of weapons systems capable of triggering an arms race in space. That is especially true of anti-satellite weaponry, air and space-based laser weapons, the placement of some elements of the missile defence system in space, and the placement in space of weaponry capable of destroying targets on Earth. However, following the election of President Barack Obama, most of those programs have been suspended. The United States has since unveiled a new national space initiative with an emphasis on developing international cooperation in space. For more details, see: *Space: Weapons, Diplomacy and Security*, ed. A. Arbatov and V. Dvorkin. Moscow: ROSSPEN, 2009. P 66-76, http://carnegieendowment.org/files/12659outer_space_ arbatov.pdf (Retrieved on September 12, 2011); news item about the report by James Clay Moltz, professor of the Naval Postgraduate School in Monterey, entitled *Changes in US Space Strategy Under President Barack Obama*, presented during a Midweek Brainstorming session at PIR Center, see http://www.pircenter.org/index.php?id= 1248&news=6111 (Retrieved on September 12, 2011); National Space Policy of the United States of America, 2010, June 28, http://www.whitehouse.gov/sites/default/files/national_space_policy_6-28-10.pdf (Retrieved on August 14, 2011).

[18] See, for example: Hansell Cristina, Potter William C. (eds.). *Engaging China and Russia on Nuclear Disarmament*. James Martin Center for Non-proliferation Studies, 2009, http://cns.miis.edu/opapers/op15/op15.pdf (Retrieved on July 14, 2011).

[19] Statement of the Government of the People's Republic of China. 1964, 16 October. http://www.nti.org/db/china/engdocs/nucsta64.htm (Retrieved on September 1, 2011).

[will] conclude an agreement to the effect that the nuclear powers and those countries which may soon become nuclear powers undertake not to use nuclear weapons either against non-nuclear countries and nuclear-free zones or against each other".[20]

Any country that has undertaken the commitment of No First Use of nuclear weapons should develop its nuclear forces based on the concept of a second (retaliatory) strike[21] – or, as the White Book puts it, the strategy of "attacking only after being attacked".[22] The main objective of such a country's nuclear policy is to make sure that its nuclear forces can deliver a retaliatory strike. In the case of China, taking into account its no-first-use commitment requires constant efforts to improve the survivability of its nuclear deterrent.

What, then, are the ways of increasing survivability? *First*, the country has to keep in secret numbers and performance, characteristics of its nuclear arsenal, as well as any plans for improving those characteristics. *Second*, it has to increase the mobility of its delivery systems. *Third*, make those delivery systems as hard as possible to detect. *Fourth*, place some of its nuclear weapons in well-protected underground silos which cannot be penetrated even by the most advanced weaponry.[23] *Fifth*, gradually increase the numbers of the delivery systems. *Sixth*, develop a reliable command-and-control system for its nuclear arsenal; most of the elements of such a system should be placed either in space or in highly protected facilities. *Finally*, such a country should always be prepared for any *strategic surprises*. At this time, these surprises include the possibility of the adversary rapidly improving its missile defence capabilities, placing weapons in space and building up the capability of its non-nuclear high-precision weapons.

---

[20] Op. Cit: Li Changhe. *Major powers and arms control: a Chinese perspective.* http://books.sipri.org/files/books/SIPRI01AnRo/SIPRI01AnRo09.pdf (Retrieved on July 2, 2011).

[21] *Nuclear Reset: Arms Reduction and Nonproliferation*, ed. A. Arbatov and V. Dvorkin. Moscow: ROSSPEN, 2011, P. 60.

[22] China's National Defence in 2010. National Defence Policy. 2011, 31 March. http://news.xinhuanet.com/english2010/china/2011-03/31/c_13806851_38.htm (Retrieved on July 2, 2011).

[23] A detailed study of the current state of the system of storage of nuclear warheads in China was completed in March 2010, by the Project2049 Institute. Stokes Mark A. *China's Nuclear Warhead Storage and Handling System*, http://www.project2049.net/documents/chinas_nuclear_warhead_storage_and_handling_system.pdf (Retrieved on July 2, 2011).

When China's nuclear doctrine was being formed the no-first-use commitment could be interpreted primarily as a political propaganda instrument; at the early stages the structure of the Chinese nuclear deterrent made it impossible to implement such a commitment in practice. However, later on, that commitment started to gain real substance, although the process is still far from complete.[24]

Several researchers have identified three stages in the evolution of China's nuclear deterrence strategy.[25]

At the first stage, China pursued the policy of so-called existential deterrence (*cunzaixing weishe*)[26]. At that point China had already acquired nuclear weapons but possessed no effective delivery systems and no real capability to deliver a retaliatory strike. In the event of a crisis it could use its nuclear weapons only against targets close to its own borders. Such a situation remained essentially unchanged until at least 1982, when the first Chinese silo-based liquid-fuel intercontinental ballistic missile, the Dongfeng-5 (DF-5) entered service. Up until that moment China's main delivery systems were the Hong-6 (H-6) strategic bomber, which was a copy of the Tu-16 made under Soviet license in China and a family of intermediate-range liquid-fuel ballistic missiles (DF-1, DF-2, DF-3 and DF-4), regarded as the first generation of Chinese missiles.[27]

---

[24] A. Arbatov argues that even at this time "the Chinese strategic nuclear forces, its missile attack early warning systems and the command-and-control and communications infrastructure are too vulnerable to ensure a retaliatory strike after a hypothetical disarming first strike by the United States or Russia." Nuclear Reset: Arms Reduction and Non-proliferation. 60.

[25] For more details, see: Chase Michael. *China's Second Artillery Corps: New Trends in Force Modernization, Doctrine, and Training.* China Brief of The Jamestown Foundation. 2007, February 27, http://www.jamestown.org/single/?no_cache=1&tx_ttnews[tt_news]=4012 (Retrieved on July 14, 2011); Fels Enrico. *Will the Eagle Strangle the Dragon? An Assessment of the US challenges towards China's nuclear deterrence, Trends East Asia,* Analysis No. 20, February 2008, www.ruhr-uni-bochum.de/oaw/poa/pdf/TEAS20.pdf *(Retrieved on July 14, 2011);* Li Bin. *Nuclear Weapons and International Relations* [Hewuqi yu guoji guanxi], briefing presented at Beijing University. 2003, November 25, learn.tsinghua.edu.cn/2000990313/nuir.pdf (Retrieved on July 20, 2011).

[26] Li Bin. Op. Cit.

[27] Shunin V. Key stages in the development of ballistic missiles in China. *Zarubezhnoye Voennoye Obozreniye.* No 7. 2009. P. 50-53.

The second stage in the evolution of China's nuclear deterrence strategy came in the late 1970s - early 1980s, when China developed its first ICBM. That made it possible for Beijing to adopt the concept of minimal deterrence (*zuidi weishe*).[28] At that stage, China already had the capability to deliver a retaliatory strike. It possessed ICBMs and intermediate-range ballistic missiles (IRBMs); any potential adversary therefore had to take into account that if some of those missiles were to survive the first strike Beijing would be able to use them to inflict unacceptable damage on the aggressor.

The beginning of the implementation of the second stage can be traced back to the 1978, when the Chinese leadership first spoke of the need for "a second generation of mobile missiles whose location can be kept secret and which would have a short time-to-launch".[29] That objective required the deployment of mobile ground-based transporter-launchers, the development of nuclear-powered submarines, armed with SLBMs and an upgrade program for strategic bombers. The Chinese leadership also made the decision to use only solid fuel technology for its future missiles (a resolution to that effect was adopted in 1983).[30] Also, the country's missile industry launched an effort to standardise the components of its ground and sea-based ICBMs and IRBMs.[31]

Speaking of China's transition to solid fuel rocket technology in the early 1980s, it has to be said that according to the results of comparative analysis of solid and liquid fuel technology (conducted more than once by various groups of specialists), each technology has its pluses and minuses. The key advantage of liquid-fuel rockets is their better energy characteristics. It means that liquid-fuel rockets can deliver more warheads to penetrate the adversary's missile defences".[32] The disadvantage of liquid-fuel missiles is that they require complex and expensive fuelling equipment. The liquid fuel itself is a highly toxic substance which poses great danger to the people

---

[28] Li Bin. Op. Cit.

[29] Ibid

[30] Ibid

[31] Yang Huan. *China's Strategic Nuclear Weapons. Chinese Views of Future Warfare.* Institute for National Strategic Studies, http://www.fas.org/nuke/guide/china/doctrine/huan.htm (Retrieved on July 14, 2011).

[32] Khramchikhin A. *Future ICBM: solid or liquid fuel? Novoye Voennoye Obozreniye.* 2011, June 17, http://nvo.ng.ru/realty/2011-06-17/1_mbr.html *(Retrieved on September 12, 2011).*

and equipment coming into contact with it.[33]

The key advantage of solid-fuel missiles is that they can be prepared for launch much quicker. Also, their launch itself is much less noisy, which is very important for nuclear missile submarines. Another advantage is that of using solid-fuel missiles.[34] Finally, the boost phase of solid-fuel missiles' trajectory is much shorter compared to liquid fuel technology (by a factor of 2 to 4), which translates into their greater ability to evade the adversary's missile defences.[35]

China's decision to use only solid-fuel technology was seen as a signal of Beijing's intention to pursue greater retaliatory strike capability of its nuclear forces by means of increasing the mobility of its ground-based ICBMs, making the future naval component of its nuclear triad harder to detect and reducing the time to launch, in the event of a nuclear conflict. On the whole, the transition to solid-fuel technology gave China greater ability to comply with its no-first-use commitment.

As part of the second stage in the late 1980s – early 1990s, China began the deployment of its first ground-based mobile solid-fuel IRBM, the DF-21, which entered service in 1991.[36] In 1988, the Chinese Navy took delivery of its first nuclear missile submarine, a Project 092 (Xia class) boat, equipped with 12 vertical launchers capable of carrying Julang-1 (JL-1) SLBMs. But that sub was inferior in many ways to similar Western boats, so it remained an experimental unit. It has never been on combat duty or left the inner Chinese waters.[37] Nevertheless, by the early 1990s the Xia and several other R&D projects had given China a solid foundation

[33] Rearmament program for Russian Strategic Missile Troops to consider both liquid-fuel and solid-fuel missiles, ARMS-TASS, February 29, 2008, http://www.militaryparitet.com/teletype/data/ic_teletype/1964/ (Retrieved on October 15, 2011)

[34] Mant D.I., Ermokhin K.M. *Those who follow in the footsteps cannot become leaders. Atomnaya Nauka.* December 26, 2008. http://www.proatom.ru/modules.php?name=News&file=print&sid=1639 (Retrieved on September 12, 2011).

[35] Khramchikhin A. *Future ICBM: solid or liquid fuel? Novoye Voennoye Obozreniye.* June 17, 2011, http://nvo.ng.ru/realty/2011-06-17/1_mbr.html *(Retrieved on September 12, 2011).*

[36] Norris Robert N., Kristensen Hans M., *Chinese Nuclear Forces 2010. The Bulletin of the Atomic Scientists*[1] 66(6). P. 134-141, http://bos.sagepub.com/content/66/6/134.full.pdf+html

[37] Fedorov V., Mosalev V. China's submarine strength. *Zarubezhnoye Voennoye Obozreniye.* No 7. 2010. P. 52-60

to develop the classic nuclear triad consisting of the land, sea and air components. The R&D focus during the second stage in the development of the Chinese nuclear arsenal was on mobile solid-fuel ground-based and sea-based missiles and on standardisation of design and engineering solutions.[38]

The third stage began in the mid 1990s and continues to this day. It is based on the concept of guaranteed minimal deterrence (*zuidi kexin weishe*)[39]. In practice, this means that China is now trying to make its retaliatory strike capability more reliable. To that end, Beijing is increasing the proportion of mobile delivery means and systems whose location can be kept secret. It is increasing the size of its nuclear arsenal at a very moderate pace, while at the same time building up its performance characteristics very rapidly. R&D projects launched during the second stage are now entering service with the Chinese nuclear forces. China has also begun to develop new types of delivery systems and is pursuing extensive upgrade projects.

One of these new R&D projects is the JL-2, a new SLMB with improved flight performance and increased range. In 2000, an upgraded version of the DF-11 tactical missile, the DF-11A (increased range) entered service with the Chinese army. Also in 2000, China launched mass production of a modified DF-15 short-range ballistic missile, the DF-15A, with greater range and an ability to manoeuvre at the final stage of the trajectory. In 2002, it started to replace the already deployed DF-21 missiles with the DF-21A modification (greater range). In 2003, the DF-31 ground-based mobile ICBM entered service, significantly reducing the strategic missile technology gap between China and the two leading nuclear powers, Russia and the United States. A further modification of the missile, the DF-31A, entered service only 3 years later, in 2006.[40]

During the same decade, China also made great progress in improving the capability of the naval component of its strategic nuclear forces. According to some sources, it also made efforts to upgrade the aviation

---

[38] Ibid
[39] Li Bin. Op. Cit.
[40] Shunin. Op. Cit.

component by equipping several H-6 and H-6M bombers with the new Changjian-20 (CJ-20) air-to-surface tactical cruise missiles capable of delivering tactical nuclear warheads.[41] In December 2002, China launched the first Project 093 (Shang Class) nuclear-powered submarine, which is based on the Russian Project 671RTM design. The submarine entered service in late 2006. The Shang Class was then used as a starting point to develop the Project 094 (Jin Class) sub. Its only difference from Project 093 is a 30 metres long missile compartment with 12 vertical launchers for the JL-2 SLBMs. Project 094 is believed to be much superior to the older Project 092 (Xia Class). It has a better nuclear power plant, more capable missiles and electronics and is less noisy compared to its predecessors. The three-stage solid-fuel JL-2 SLBM shares many components with the DF-31 ICBM and can carry a single nuclear warhead with a yield of up to 1,000 kt. According to some sources, China is now developing a MIRVed head section for this SLBM (three 100 kt warheads).[42] The first test launches of the JL-2 were held in July 2004, but they were largely unsuccessful and the current operational state of that SLBM is unclear.[43]

As of early 2011, China's nuclear forces included a land-based, sea-based and air-based components, with both strategic and non-strategic delivery systems (see Table 1). After comparing data from various open sources, it can be said with a fair degree of confidence that the Chinese nuclear arsenal now includes about 240 strategic delivery systems and about 375 non-strategic systems.[44] The overall number of Chinese warheads (deployed and in storage) that can be mounted on strategic delivery systems

---

[41] China's CJ-20 Air Launched Cruise Missile to be operational with H-6 Bomber, Pakistan Defence, December 07, 2009, http://www.defence.pk/forums/china-defence/40868-china-s-cj-20-air-launched-cruise-missile-operational-h-6-bomber.html (Retrieved on October 15, 2011)

[42] Nuclear weapons and national security. Rosatom Institute of Strategic Stability. Saransk: Red October Printing House, 2008, P 105, http://www.iss-atom.ru/book-22/nuc_weap_iss.pdf (Retrieved on October 15, 2011)

[43] Fedorov V., Mosalev V. Op. Cit.

[44] For more details about the development of strategic and non-strategic nuclear weapons see, for example: A. Arbatov. *Tactical Nuclear Weapons: Problems and Solutions, Nezavisimoye Voennoye Obozreniye*, May 20, 2011, http://nvo.ng.ru/concepts/2011-05-20/1_nuclear.html (Retrieved on October 17, 2011)

is about 260.[45]

Table 1. China's nuclear arsenal in 2010

Type of delivery system (Chinese and NATO designation)	Number of deployed delivery systems	Range (km)	Number of warheads carried and yield	First deployed	Number of deployed warheads
STRATEGIC DELIVERY SYSTEMS					~180
DF-4 (CSS-3) - liquid-fuel two-stage IRBM, mobile and silo-based	15-20	5.400	1 x 3.3 Mt	1980	~20
DF-5A (CSS-4 Mod 2) - liquid-fuel ICBM, silo-based	~20	13.000+	1 x 4-5 Mt	1981	~20
DF-21 (CSS-5) and modifications [46] - mobile solid-fuel IRBM (regional deterrence)	85-95	1.750+	1 x 200-300 kt	1991	~95
DF-31 (CSS-9) - mobile solid-fuel three-stage ICBM	10+	7.200+	1 ? 200-300 kt	2003	~10

[45] These calculations and information in the table are based on the following sources: Shunin V. Op. Cit.; Annual Report to Congress. Military and Security Developments Involving the People's Republic of China. May 6, 2011, http://www.defence.gov/pubs/pdfs/2011_cmpr_final.pdf (Retrieved on June 1, 2011); Norris Robert N., Kristensen Hans M. Op. Cit.; *The Military Balance 2010*. The International Institute for Strategic Studies, 2010. P. 398-408. Nuclear weapons and national security. Rosatom Institute of Strategic Stability. Saransk: Red October Printing House, 2008, P 105, http://www.iss-atom.ru/book-22/nuc_weap_iss.pdf (Retrieved on October 15, 2011). China's National Defence in 2008. Information Office of the State Council of the People's Republic of China. Beijing, January 29, 2009. – P. 27-43. URL: http://merln.ndu.edu/whitepapers/China_English2008.pdf (Retrieved on October 15, 2011). Stokes M. China's nuclear warhead storage and handling system / Project 2049 Institute. March 12, 2010. – 21 p. URL: http://project2049.net/documents/chinas_nuclear_warhead_storage_and_handling_system.pdf (Retrieved on November 7, 2010). *The Military Balance 2010*. The International Institute for Strategic Studies, 2010. – pp. 398-408.

[46] This table also takes into account modified delivery systems capable of carrying both nuclear and conventional warheads. However, some papers do not count these dual-use delivery systems towards the overall tally.

DF-31A (CSS-9 Mod 2) - mobile solid-fuel ICBM	10-15	11.200+	1 ? 200-300 kt	2008-2010	~15
JL-1 (CSS-N-3) - SLBM (1 Xia Class nuclear missile sub, not fully deployed)	(12)[47]	1.770+	1 ? 25-50 kt	1986	(12)
JL-2 (CSS-NX-5) - SLBM (up to 5 Jin Class nuclear missile subs at various stages of assembly or deployment)	(60)	7.200+	1 ? 100 kt [48]	2012?x [49]	(60)
H-6 (and modifications) - bomber [50]	~82	3.100+	Up to 3 B-5 bombs ? 2 Mt	1965	~20
NON-STRATEGIC DELIVERY SYSTEMS [51]					?
Qiang-5 (and modifications) - fighter-bomber [52]	~120	Up to 400	1 bomb ? 5-20 kt	1972	?
CJ-10 (DH-10)	45-55	1.500+	1 ??	2007	?
surface-to-surface cruise missile					

[47] Most experts believe that the JL-1 and JL-2 SLBMs have not yet become fully operational. The Navy section of China's National Defence 2008 White Book (p. 32) claims that "the Chinese Navy has several nuclear missile submarines". In this table, the nuclear warheads and delivery systems, presumably carried by the Chinese nuclear missile submarines are not counted towards the overall tally of nuclear warheads and delivery systems.

[48] Several open sources claim that the new JL-2 SLBMs can be armed with MIRVed head sections with 3 or 4 warheads.

[49] According to some reports, tests of the missile are in progress.

[50] Several modifications of this bomber have been developed in China, but all of them were very similar to the Tu-16. Production ended in 1994. The project to develop a new bomber, which was launched quite a while ago, is still stuck at the engineering design stage.

[51] Information about China's non-strategic nuclear weapons is limited and contradictory. Non-strategic nuclear weapons are in service with the Second Artillery Force, the Army and frontline (tactical) aviation.

[52] This fighter-bomber is a deeply upgraded version of the MiG-19, which China used to assembly under Soviet license (designated as the J-6). Mass production of the Q-5 fighter-bomber began in the 1970s. Following the acquisition of tactical nuclear weapons, Beijing also launched a project to develop a modification of the Q-5 capable of carrying nuclear bombs with an estimated yield of 5-20 kt. The aircraft, which is still in production, has undergone several waves of upgrades. The new Q-7 fighter-bomber is being developed to replace the Q-5, but for now there is no information as to whether it will be used as a delivery system for nuclear weapons.

| DF-15 (CSS-6) - SRBM [53] | 90-110 | 600 | 1x? | 1995 | ? |
| DF-11A (CSS-7) - tactical missile | 120-140 | 300-450 | 1x? | 2000 | ? |

In the future, China is likely to continue its efforts aimed at improving its guaranteed minimal deterrence capability by means of further increasing the proportion of mobile and hidden delivery systems in its nuclear arsenal. The quantitative size of the Chinese strategic nuclear forces is likely to continue its moderate growth. Beijing will probably continue to develop new delivery systems and upgrade the existing ones. In any event, experts believe that at present, China does not yet have adequate nuclear capability to underpin its no-first-use obligation to the full extent and without damage to the implementation of the country's nuclear strategy.

American Missile Defence System and Prospects for a Reduction of Chinese Nuclear Arsenal

The second obstacle preventing China from joining the nuclear disarmament process is the deployment of the US global missile defence system.

In 1972, the Soviet Union and the United States signed the Treaty on the Limitation of Anti-Ballistic Missile Systems. The treaty was based on the recognition of the fact that ABM systems can undermine strategic stability if they protect a country's territory from a massive nuclear strike by intercepting a large proportion of attacking missiles and warheads. If, on the other hand, ABM systems protect only ICBM, SLBM and strategic aviation bases and the upper tiers of command-and-control systems, they can strengthen strategic stability.[54] That is why Washington's decision to withdraw from the ABM Treaty in 2002 and to reject any restrictions on the development of missile defence systems can undermine international strategic stability. That stability is based "not on quantitative parity of strategic weapons but on the parity of the two sides' capability to inflict

---

[53] The Second Artillery Force includes at least five active SRBM brigades. Another two brigades are serving with the Army; one is stationed in Nanjing Military District, another in Guangzhou Military District. All the Chinese SRBMs are deployed in the immediate vicinity of the Taiwan Strait.

[54] Nuclear Reset: Arms Reduction and Non-proliferation. p. 31.

guaranteed unacceptable damage on the adversary in a retaliatory strike, no matter how the nuclear conflict unfolds."[55]

China, which has a limited number of nuclear warheads and delivery systems, is now faced with the deployment of elements of the US missile defence system nearby the Chinese borders. That represents a serious challenge to China's nuclear deterrence capability. At present, Beijing has about 40 ICBMs capable of reaching the US mainland.[56] In the event of a hypothetical nuclear exchange between the United States and China at least some of those ICBMs will be taken out by the first strike, given American technological superiority in nuclear and high-precision weapons.[57] The US missile defence system, capable of intercepting the Chinese missiles which survive the first strike would make the Chinese nuclear strategy incapable of ensuring the country's national security.

Since Washington's withdrawal from the ABM Treaty the United States "has made great progress in improving its multi-layer missile defence system in Asia Pacific; that system can now intercept any type of ballistic missiles, of any range, and at any phase of their trajectory (boost, midcourse and terminal)."[58] At this moment, the American missile defence system in Asia Pacific "includes reconnaissance and information early warning means such as strategic radars capable of detecting ICBMs at a range of over 5,500km, as well as land and sea-based interceptors".[59]

The United States is also providing assistance to its key allies in the region (primarily Japan, Australia and South Korea, as well as Taiwan) in developing tactical missile defence systems and potentially, strategic missile defences. Japan already has a multi-layer missile defence system consisting

---

[55] Development of forward-based elements of the American missile defence system: technological aspects and possible response measures. *Indeks Bezopasnosti*. No. 1 (88), Vol. 15. P. 75-93.

[56] Kallmyer Kevin. *START and China: Really?* Center for Strategic and International Studies. 2010, September 23, http://csis.org/blog/start-and-china-really (Retrieved on August 14, 2011).

[57] Li Bin. The Impact of the U.S. NMD on the Chinese Nuclear Modernisation, http://www.emergingfromconflict.org/readings/bin.pdf (Retrieved on July 20, 2011).

[58] Kozin V. *US missile defence system: Eastern European system being adjusted, the Asian system being ramped up? Natsionalnaya Oborona*. No 12. December 2010, http://old.nationaldefence.ru/283/308/index.shtml?id=3894# *(Retrieved on September 12, 2011).*

[59] Ibid

of tracking systems, interceptors, early warning systems and a command-and-control system.[60] Also, the United States and Japan are jointly developing the next generation of interceptors, the SM-3 Block IIA, which is to be deployed, starting from 2018. Australia is acquiring ships which can be made compatible with the Aegis system. Meanwhile, South Korea and the United States are conducting a joint assessment of missile threats in the region.[61]

Theoretically there are at least two ways of reducing the threat posed by the American missile defence system in Asia Pacific to China's nuclear deterrence capability. The most obvious way is rapidly increasing the size of the Chinese nuclear arsenal by building more of the existing missile types and developing new ones, capable of penetrating missile defences. That includes missiles equipped with MIRVed and highly manoeuvrable warheads.[62] The DoD believes that by 2015, China's nuclear forces will include an additional number of the DF-31A ICBMs and improved DF-5A missiles.[63]

But if China chooses this path, it will have to expend significant financial resources. Given the proclaimed task of "coordinated development of the economy and national defence"[64] this could have a serious negative impact on the Chinese economy. Second, such a course of action would inevitably trigger a new wave of alarm over the Chinese threat and damage China's existing positive image in the area of nuclear non-proliferation.[65] Third, any program to build large numbers of new warheads would require

[60] Statement of Dr. James N. Miller, Principal Deputy Under Secretary of Defence for Policy before the House Committee on Armed Services Subcommittee on Strategic Forces. March 2, 2011, http://armedservices.house.gov/index.cfm/files/serve?File_id=10a50d6f-ece1-475f-bb5e-00ab478aefdb (Retrieved on May 14, 2011).

[61] Ibid

[62] Li Bin. *The Impact of the U.S. NMD on the Chinese Nuclear Modernisation.*

[63] Annual Report to Congress. *Military and Security Developments Involving the People's Republic of China 2011*, May 6, 2011. P. 44. http://www.defence.gov/pubs/pdfs/2011_cmpr_final.pdf (Retrieved on June 1, 2011).

[64] China's National Defence in 2008. Information Office of the State Council of the People's Republic of China. Beijing. 2009, January 29. P. 9, http://merln.ndu.edu/whitepapers/China_English2008.pdf (Retrieved on September 15, 2011).

[65] Warden John, Yun He. *US Missile Defence and China: An Exchange. PacNet* ¹50. 2011, September 6, http://csis.org/files/publication/pac1150.pdf (Retrieved on September 14, 2011).

an additional amount of fissile material. That would push back even further, the potential time frame for China's constructive involvement in negotiating a ban on the production of fissile materials for weapons purposes. It might even make fresh nuclear tests by China necessary,[66] making it impossible for the Comprehensive Nuclear Test Ban Treaty (CTBT) to enter into force.[67] Another thing to keep in mind is China's long-standing pledge never to participate in a nuclear arms race and to maintain its nuclear arsenal at a minimally sufficient level to ensure its national security.[68]

In any event, if China were to build up its nuclear arsenal, that would have negative effects for the entire system of regional security in Asia Pacific. Faced with such a scenario, Japan and South Korea might try to acquire their own nuclear capability. Such a move by China could also trigger a nuclear arms race between India and Pakistan[69] and have a very adverse impact on Russian-Chinese strategic dialogue. Besides, a rapid increase in the numbers of Chinese nuclear weapons would disturb the strategic balance in Asia Pacific, prompting the United States and its allies to speed up their missile defence deployment in the region.

Finally, a sharp increase in the size of the Chinese nuclear arsenal would probably mean that Beijing has abandoned its current defensive posture, including its no-first-use commitment. At the very least, that commitment would become more of a propaganda tool than a practical strategy. Such an increase could signal a transition to the "launch under attack" strategy, whereby Beijing would try to reduce to a minimum, the time between the enemy's strike and the launch of its own nuclear missiles. That would require advanced and highly reliable early warning systems - which, according to various sources, China either does not have at all or is only just beginning to deploy. According to some sources, at present China

---

[66] Li Bin. *The Impact of the U.S. NMD on the Chinese Nuclear Modernisation.*

[67] In future China could become much less dependent on test detonations of nuclear devices to improve their combat characteristics. This is thanks largely to the rapid development of supercomputer technologies in China, which are a critical element of the so-called *nuclear tests in a lab* infrastructure. For details on the development of such supercomputers in China see, for example: Yonck Richard. *The Supercomputer Race.* 26 September, 2010, http://www.wfs.org/content/supercomputer-race (Retrieved on December 12, 2010).

[68] China's National Defence in 2010. Arms Control and Disarmament. 31.03.2011. http://news.xinhuanet.com/english2010/china/2011-03/31/c_13806851_38.htm (Retrieved on July 2, 2011).

[69] Fels Enrico. Op. Cit. p. 9

stores nuclear warheads separately from the missiles. A number of researchers believe this is because China "lacks reliable technical means for preventing unauthorised use of nuclear weapons".[70]

The second path, which China is more likely to take, is to continue strengthening its guaranteed minimal deterrence capability. In practice, that would translate into further efforts to increase the proportion of mobile delivery systems in the Chinese nuclear arsenal and developing various measures to defeat missile defence systems, including MIRVed manoeuvrable warheads and anti-satellite weapons.[71] If China chooses this option, it will continue increasing the quantitative size of its nuclear arsenal at a *moderate* pace and pursue upgrade programs for weapons systems already in service. It will also focus on developing the naval component of its strategic nuclear triad to make sure that its nuclear weapons are mobile and hard to detect, while also abiding by its no-first-use commitment.[72]

According to some sources, by 2020, China can deploy up to five Project 094 (Jin Class) nuclear missile submarines.[73] Nevertheless, even if all five are successfully deployed, these subs will be able to deliver a guaranteed retaliatory strike against the United States only if they conduct their patrols relatively far away from the Chinese coast.[74] That will require adequate defences against the adversary's anti-submarine measures in open seas.[75] At present, the Chinese Navy is no match for the American naval strength. The naval component of the Chinese nuclear triad has always

---

[70] *Nuclear Reset: Arms Reduction and Non-proliferation.* P. 60.

[71] Annual Report to Congress. *Military and Security Developments Involving the People's Republic of China.* 2011, May 6. P. 44, http://www.defence.gov/pubs/pdfs/2011_cmpr_final.pdf (Retrieved on June 1, 2011).

[72] See, for example: Yoshihara Toshi, Holmes James R., "China's New Undersea Nuclear Deterrent, Strategy, Doctrine, and Capabilities." *Joint Force Quarterly.* 2008, July, http://www.usnwc.edu/getattachment/Research—Gaming/China-Maritime-Studies-Institute/Published-Articles/JFQ_ChineseSSBN_YoshiharaHolmes.pdf (Retrieved on September 17, 2011).

[73] Chuprin Konstantin. *The Great Underwater Wall. Novosti VPK.* June 22, 2010. http://vpk.name/news/40613_velikaya_podvodnaya_stena.html (Retrieved on July 12, 2011).

[74] Chinese Responses to U.S. Military Transformation and Implications for the Department of Defencå. RAND Corporation, 2006, http://www.rand.org/pubs/monographs/2006/RAND_MG340.pdf (Retrieved on June 1, 2011).

[75] For details on the development of Chinese anti-submarine defences, see: Stokes Mark A. China's Evolving Conventional Strategic Strike Capability: the Anti-ship Ballistic Missile Challenge to U.S. Maritime Operations in the Western Pacific and Beyond. Project2049 Institute, 2009, September 14, http://project2049.net/documents/chinese_anti_ship_ballistic_missile_ asbm.pdf (Retrieved on August 15, 2011).

lagged behind the other two components. For that reason, the Chinese military have little experience in conducting such operations. Meanwhile, the US Navy is constantly improving its capability versus the navies of potential adversaries.[76] What is more, if the American missile defence system in Asia Pacific acquires sufficient capability versus the adversary's missiles, the threat to the Chinese Navy from the American one will increase even further; by containing the Chinese submarines in one geographic area, the US Navy would be able to target its missile defences against China's main naval strength.[77]

The New START-A View From China

The New START treaty between Russia and the United States entered into force on February 5, 2011. It limits the number of deployed strategic nuclear warheads to 1,550 apiece. The ceiling for deployed ICBMs, deployed SLBMs and deployed strategic bombers has been set at 700 apiece. Immediately after the signing of the new treaty, some experts and politicians in both Russia and the US began to say that the time has come to involve the other nuclear powers, especially China, in the nuclear disarmament process. They argue that China remains the only official nuclear weapon state which, rather than reducing its nuclear arsenal, actually continues to increase it. They also pointed out that within the next decade, the size of the Chinese nuclear arsenal is expected to reach the Russian and US levels.[78]

Chinese experts, meanwhile, saw the signing of the New START treaty as an achievement limited mainly to Russian-US relations. They said the treaty reflected "a consensus achieved by the two largest nuclear powers".[79] They were quite optimistic about the prospects for the treaty's

---

[76] Chinese Responses to U.S. Military Transformation and Implications for the Department of Defence.

[77] Fels Enrico. Op. Cit. p. 11.

[78] See, for example: Peter Brookes, New START Treaty's China Challenge, New York Post, September 20, 2010, http://www.nypost.com/p/news/opinion/opedcolumnists/new_start_treaty_china_challenge_5niHZQbbup6tknXsyjN2II (Retrieved on August 10, 2011); Kallmyer Kevin , *START and China: Really?*; Stokes Mark, Blumenthal Dan. *Why China's missiles should be our focus. The Washington Post.* 2011, January 2, http://www.washingtonpost.com/wp-dyn/content/article/2010/12/31/AR2010123102687.html (Retrieved on August 12, 2011).

implementation when it entered into force. But they also said the document had some clear drawbacks, including the fact that it "limits only the deployed warheads and does not cover the warheads in storage". They also regretted that "the treaty does not address the problem of tactical nuclear weapons or conventional weapons; nor does it limit the deployment of missile defence systems". Taking into account such views on the New START treaty expressed by Chinese experts, it would be too soon to expect any significant progress on China joining the nuclear disarmament process in the near future.[80] The above mentioned White Paper, which was released in March 2011, after the entry into force of the New START treaty, only repeats China's calls on Russia and the United States to continue reducing their nuclear arsenals; the new treaty itself is not even mentioned in the document.[81]

Also, even though Chinese experts have been fairly optimistic about the prospects for the implementation of the new treaty, Russian and American politicians have since made plenty of statements that can weaken such optimism. It is important to remember the ongoing confrontation between the two countries over Washington's plans to station elements of its global missile defence system in Europe.

As for China's repeated demands for Russia and the United States to achieve significant reductions of their nuclear arsenals, it is not clear how deep those reductions should be to satisfy Beijing.[82] Some say that bringing the two countries' holdings of nuclear warheads to about 1,000 should be enough for China to consider joining the nuclear disarmament process in a multilateral format.[83] Others believe that the necessary level is 800 warheads, i.e. 3 times as many as China currently has.[84] Still others argue that China cannot participate in a phased nuclear disarmament process at all because its nuclear arsenal is too small as it is. They say that for China,

---

[79] US-Russia nuke treaty «good for global stability». *China Daily*. 2011, January 28, 2011, http://www.chinadaily.com.cn/cndy/2011-01/28/content_11930816.htm (Retrieved on July 14, 2011).

[80] Ibid.

[81] China's National Defence in 2010. Arms Control and Disarmament.

[82] Bates Gill. China and *Nuclear Arms Control: Current Positions and Future Policies. SIPRI Insights on Peace and Security*. 2010, 4 April, http://books.sipri.org/files/insight/ SIPRIInsight1004.pdf (Retrieved on August 14, 2011).

a more feasible approach might be to set a ceiling to be later followed by complete elimination.[85] In other words, even if the New START treaty is implemented successfully and on schedule, China is unlikely to be ready for reducing its own nuclear arsenal by 2020.

Will There be Cuts?

So, the final conclusion would be that it seems unlikely that in the next decade China will show any willingness to reduce its strategic nuclear arsenal. There are many reasons for that, both external and internal.

The main internal reason is China's strategy of strengthening its guaranteed minimal deterrence capability by increasing the proportion of mobile and hidden delivery means and developing countermeasures against the potential adversary's missile defences, including MIRVed warheads. Beijing will continue to increase the number of its nuclear weapons at a moderate pace and carry on with upgradation of programs for the existing weaponry. Most experts agree that over the next decade China will not acquire adequate deterrence capability to underpin its long-standing no-first-use policy. The country will therefore continue to increase the size of its strategic nuclear arsenal at a moderate pace until that capability is sufficient for the purposes of no-first-use.

The external factors include the deployment of missile defence systems in Asia Pacific and the outcome of the US-Russian bilateral disarmament process.

In reference to missile defences, the most likely scenario is that China will not seek to build up its strategic nuclear arsenal in response to the deployment of BMD systems in Asia Pacific. Such a step would have too many negative effects for the security situation in the region and for China

---

[83] Shen, D., 'China's nuclear perspective: deterrence reduction, nuclear non-proliferation, and disarmament', *Strategic Analysis*, vol. 32, no. 4 (July 2008), p. 643, http://www.tandfonline.com/doi/abs/10.1080/09700160802214409 (Retrieved on October 15, 2011)

[84] Bates Gill. *China and Nuclear Arms Control: Current Positions and Future Policies.*

[85] Li B., 'China: a crucial bridge for the 2005 NPT Review Conference', *Arms Control Today*, vol. 35, no. 1, January/February 2005, http://www.armscontrol.org/act/2005_01-02/Li (Retrieved on October 15, 2011)

itself. Increasing the size of the Chinese nuclear arsenal at a moderate pace while at the same time improving its performance characteristics would be an adequate response; it would also be in line with China's no-first-use policy. But unless the American missile defence system in Asia Pacific is dismantled, or unless some way of establishing US-Chinese cooperation on missile defence is found, Beijing will not join the nuclear disarmament process any time soon.

Finally, about the nuclear disarmament process in the bilateral US-Russian format and of China's reaction to it, one has to take into account that even if the New START treaty is implemented successfully and on schedule, China is unlikely to cut its own strategic nuclear forces after 2020. What is more, it is hard to see China taking part in multilateral nuclear disarmament after 2020 even if the United States and Russia reduce their arsenals *below* the ceilings agreed in the new treaty. There is a strong likelihood that even in such a situation, some of the nuclear-weapon states will refuse to adopt the no-first-use policy and that China and the United States will be unable to find a joint solution to the problem of missile defences in Asia Pacific.

Contributors

Mr. Sverre Lodgaard is currently Senior Research Fellow at the Norwegian Institute of International Affairs. He was formerly, Director of NUPI 1997–2007. He is engaged in the projects *Non-profileration*[2] and *Doables in the Field of Nuclear Disarmament* of the Institute[3].

Ambassador T.P. Sreenivasan was formerly Permanent Representative of India to the United Nations, Vienna and Governor for India of the International Atomic Energy Agency, Vienna and Ambassador to Austria and Slovenia (2000-2004). Mr. Sreenivasan is presently a member of the National Security Advisory Board of the Government of India, the Director General, Kerala International Centre

Dr. Bruno Tertrais is a Senior Research Fellow at the Fondation pour la Recherche Strategique (FRS). He graduated from the Institut d'études politiques de Paris in 1984. He holds a Master's degree in Public Law (1985) and a Doctorate in Political Science (1994). He is a member of the International Institute for Strategic Studies and a member of the editorial board of the Washington Quarterly.

Ambassador Jacek Bylica is Head of the WMD Non-Proliferation Centre in NATO. He was Security Policy Director at the Ministry of Foreign Affaires, Poland, and for several years Director of the Asia-Pacific Department. The WMD Centre was established in May 2000 as a result of the 1999 Washington Summit WMD Initiative with the aim of supporting Alliance political and military efforts to improve the overall response to the proliferation of WMD and their means of delivery.

Lt. Gen. (Retd.) Prakash Menon, PVSM, AVSM, VSM, PhD, has been commandant of the National Defence College, New Delhi for the past two years. He is a member of the expert group on Indian National Defence University (INDU). He is currently with the National Security Council Secretariat.

Dr. Swaran Singh is Chairperson, Centre for International Politics, Organization and Disarmament, School of International Studies, Jawaharlal Nehru University. He has research and publications experience of over 20 years on issues of Arms Control and Disarmament, War and Peace, Defence, Security and Nuclear issues, on China's foreign and security policies, especially on India-China and India-Pakistan Confidence Building Measures; more recently evolved special interest in teaching and research on Peace and Conflict Resolution.

Dr. G. Balachandran is a Consulting Fellow at the IDSA. He is associated with the National Maritime Foundation, New Delhi. He is a Consultant both to the Americas Division of the Indian Ministry of External Affairs and to the CII. Dr. Balachandran has conducted studies and published widely on the *India-United States Next Steps in Strategic Partnership* as well as on *India-US Civil Nuclear Co-operation Agreement*.

Dr. Ian Anthony

Research Coordinator and Director of the SIPRI Programme on Arms Control, Disarmament and Non-proliferation. He has published numerous books on issues related to arms control, disarmament and export control.

Dr. Sheel Kant Sharma

Dr. Sharma was India's Ambassador to Austria and Permanent Representative to IAEA from 2004 to 2008. He has also been Secretary-General of SAARC, and is currently SAF Advisor to FICCI.

Mr. Alexander Kolbin

A graduate from the Tomsk State University. He has been a participant in several international conferences on international security and nuclear nonproliferation. His research interests include transatlantic relations and European security.

www.ingramcontent.com/pod-product-compliance
Lightning Source LLC
Chambersburg PA
CBHW060839100426
42814CB00016B/425/J